WHO IS THIS ALLAH?

by G.J.O. Moshay

Dorchester House Publications

Dorchester House Publications
Gerrards Cross
Bucks SL9 8HA
U.K.

Second Edition October 1995

ISBN 0 9518386 1 X

CONTENTS

NOTES

Many translations of the Quran have been compared especially against the two most authoritative ones, *Quran: Text, Translation and Commentary* by A. Yusuf Ali and the translation of Drs M. Al-Hilali and M. Muhsin Kahn of the Islamic University, Medina. The problem faced when comparing verses of different translations is that the numbering of some of the verses is not the same. The verse system used is that of A. Yusuf Ali which is the one commonly used in Islamic countries. In the 1989 edition of A. Yusuf Ali's translation some verse numbers have been changed from this system. Despite these differences in numbering we have not observed any differences in the Arabic text. Unless otherwise indicated quotations are from A. Yusuf Ali, 1938 edition.

The King James Authorised version of the Bible has been used throughout.

FOREWORD

When this book appeared in 1990 it seemed, to a number of us in Europe and the USA, that it addressed one of the most important issues of the day. Since then it has been widely circulated, particularly in Nigeria where it was first published, and has also proved a great stimulus in the debate concerning the Allah of Islam.

The debate has relevance to Christian attitudes to Islam and to Muslim attitudes to Christianity. It is also of importance to the lawmakers of societies who seek to accommodate the needs and aspirations of Muslims where, previously, Christianity has been the main influence upon the laws of a country. It is necessary, for example, that the God of Islam is understood by those who are reviewing the laws of blasphemy in Britain, and by others who are responsible for the teaching of religious topics in schools, and still others who must make decisions regarding the building of mosques in a variety of our communities.

Many people in the West have little knowledge of Islam, and many Muslims have not been taught the difference between the teaching of the Bible and the teaching of the Quran. Hence this book is timely for both Muslims and Christians. A number of Christian leaders have checked the book for its accuracy and appropriateness for distribution in the West, and thoroughly endorse the message that it contains. G.J.O. Moshay has written from the background of understanding and experience in Nigeria, and this adds much weight to the message. The book has been revised with the European and American reader in mind, without losing any of the essential detail of the original publication.

It is recommended for a wide readership of both Muslims and non-Muslims, so that in all cases the truth about Allah can be understood.

Dr Clifford Denton
October 1993

PREFACE

Whether Sunnism, Sufism, Shi'itism, Wahhabism, Ahmadiyya, Bahai Faith, or any one of the one hundred and fifty sects of Islam, the common denominator is 'Allah'. But, *Who is this Allah?*

Much has been written, and still is being written on the religion of Islam and its prophet; but not much has been written about its God. One reason is possibly because of the general assumption that the God of Islam and the God of Christianity are one and the same. Another reason might be that if this assumption proved to be incorrect it would cause many problems. The issue is indeed problematical but the solution is important to both Muslims and Christians. For example if Allah is God and the Quran true, then the Christian can be sure he is lost — no matter how zealous he may be; the reverse case would prove equally disastrous.

It is necessary, therefore, to determine sufficient facts and information to enable the reader to arrive at his own verdict, and answer the question: *Who is this Allah?*

I have many friends among Muslims and I can bear witness that they are zealous, even more zealous than many professing Christians. My prayer is that the Muslim reader will use his zeal to journey with me patiently and prayerfully through these pages, as we look forward to a better understanding of our faith and the One we are serving with all our zeal. If there are any areas which cause offence I assure the reader that it is not intentional.

"Consider what I say; and the Lord give thee understanding in all things." (2 Timothy 2:7)

G.J.O Moshay

CHAPTER ONE

Introduction

"Blessed is the nation whose God is the LORD" (Psalm 33:12).
(And blessed is the religion whose God is the Lord).

THERE is this story of a man who, during an election campaign rally, had on his car bumper, a sticker with the inscription: **"My mind is already made up — don't confuse me with the facts."** Many of us are guilty of adopting this attitude towards beliefs that we hold. We take comfort by ignoring any facts which we find confusing or disturbing. This attitude is dangerous; especially when those 'facts' concern the salvation of one's soul.

For a long time it has been assumed that Christians and Muslims serve the same God, and that they only differ in their language of expression and mode of worship. However, after fourteen centuries of history and in the light of our present-day experiences, it has now become necessary for us to undertake a systematic study of the deity of Allah and search for the real identity of the Muslim God. This is the 'raison d'être' for this book.

The seriousness of this issue demands outright candour; but we wish to stress that this book has been written not out of bitterness or resentment against Muslims, but out of the Christian love by which we are constrained to speak the truth to the general reader, and to our beloved Muslim friends in particular so that we can be bold on the day of judgment for having risked our very lives to discuss this important matter:

"Herein is our love made perfect, that we may have boldness in the day of judgment... There is no fear in love; but perfect love casteth out fear" (1 John 4:17-18).

Who Is Allah?

A number of thoughtful people have often asked: Is Allah God? Is he the *"God and the Father of our Lord Jesus Christ"* (Colossians 1:3)? Many opinions abound. Some have said Allah is simply God — the same God of the Bible as He is known in the Arabic language. Some say he cannot possibly be; they say they do not know who he is, but that they are sure he is different from the God of the Bible. Some say he is indeed a mighty god, but not the Almighty God. Yet some believe that there are two Allahs. They say the 'Allah' of the Arab and Hausa Christians is different from the 'Allah' of the Muslims. According to them, while the Allah of the Arab Christians is God, the Allah of the Muslims is not. But if he is not, who is he?

This issue of the identity of Allah has oscillated now for a number of years, and it is time we dug up some bare bone facts and determined the truth of the matter. A lie engineered by the devil cannot be defeated by hazy and vague ideas. In matters like these that concern the salvation of man's soul, there can be no substitute for the truth. Half truths are dangerous. We must go deep into the Quran, Hadith, history, linguistics and back to the Bible to get adequate information on this topic.

We need to stress that there can be no other source of the history of Islam except from the Muslim historians themselves, especially as contained in the Islamic Traditions called the Hadith. These Traditions are many and voluminous and a study of them can be tortuous. But since there is no alternative to adequate information, we must consult these works.

Not all Sunnas and Hadiths (see Appendix) are accepted by all Muslims as authentic. Therefore, we shall endeavour not to quote any tradition that contradicts the Quran in any place. Those quoted shall be only to explain further what has been said in the Quran. The major and generally accepted Hadiths to both Shiites and Sunnis are the *Mazalim* or Sahih Al Bukhari, *Kitab al zakat* by Muslim, Sahih Muslim, *Mishkatu'l Masabih, Surat'ur Rasul* by Ibn Ishaq, and those of Ibn Athir, Abu Daud, Abu c Abd ar-Rahmann-al-Nasa and Abu c Isa Mohammed, Jami'at Tirmidhi, Ibn Majah and Sunna An-Nasa'i.

A cosmetic treatment of this matter would achieve nothing and could only lead to a conclusion that is more confusing than convincing, and as a result, dangerous concerning the destiny of the many millions of souls of well-meaning adherents of Islam. Consequently this will be an indepth study and every effort will be made to anticipate all brain-boiling questions that may be raised.

Muslims have generally been reluctant to use the English word for God, and have preferred 'Allah'. The substitution of 'God' for 'Allah' only compounds the issue before us. To believe there is no difference between the two is too simplistic. What does the Quran say about this?

Speaking to the Christians and the Jews of his time who had some reservations on the object of worship in Islam, Mohammed said, "Our God and your God is One; and it is to Him we bow". (Surah 29:46; 3:84). That is, 'the Allah we bow to in Islam and the Jehovah of your Bible are the same being.'

It may be easy for many people to accept this claim. But a serious truth-seeking Christian or Muslim who refuses to accept things as they appear on the surface, and carefully studies the Quran and compares it with the Bible, soon discovers that the truth is not as simple as claimed. That great scholar of Islamic religion, Samuel Zwemer, wrote: "It is so easy to be misled by a name or by etymologies. Nearly all writers take for granted that the God of the Koran is the same being and has like attributes

11

as Jehovah or as the Godhead of the New Testament. Is this view correct?" A big question indeed!

Since this question was asked back in 1905, much research work has been undertaken. Now, with the century running out, we need to settle the question once and for all. This may not go down well with some people — especially when they are discussing inter-faithism and closing their eyes as to what divides the religions of the world. Dr Robert Morey says, "The sloppy thinking that would ignore the essential differences which divide world religions is an insult to the uniqueness of world religions"

As said in the Preface, this theme may not be as simple as some of us might think. And in order to avoid the problems and confusion that the issue entails, a Christian professor of Islamic theology, Kenneth Cragg, in his apologetic, *The Call of the Minaret*, says: "Those who say that Allah is not 'the God and Father of our Lord Jesus Christ' are right if they mean that God is not so described by Muslims. They are wrong if they mean that Allah is other than the God of the Christian faith."[1] On the surface, this observation seems to have settled the matter; but we do not think the issue is so simple as to be dismissed in those two sentences. The problem lies in the origin of the Quran. Are the claims in the Quran mere apprehensions of the Divine from the Muslims' heads? Was the message in the Quran received or conceived?

One thing we must understand as we proceed in this discussion is that, although there could be a philosophy of religion, religion itself, basically, is not a philosophy but a revelation. It cannot be judged on the same plane as the Platonic, Socratic, Cartesian or

1 Cragg, Kenneth, *The Call of the Minaret*, Wm Collins Sons & Co., London, 1986, p.30.

other philosophies. Islam, in particular, is a religion of revelation (ARABIC: *wahy or naql*), at least at its inception. It would be helpful for us to realize that the difference or otherwise between Allah and the God of the Christian faith is not merely one of description as Professor Cragg suggests.

Muslims do not say they are describing Allah. In fact, Allah cannot be described. All a Muslim can do is to raise his hands to the sky or bow down in adoration and say, 'Allahu Akbar'! He is too great to be described by human beings. Even his "99 Most Beautiful Names" in the Quran are not descriptions by human beings. They are revelations by Allah himself. Mohammed did not just rise up to conceive of the Allah in the Quran. Conception is a person's own idea about a thing (ARABIC: *aql*); it is a product of man.

According to Muslims and the Quran, Islam did not originate from Mohammed's consciousness. He might have had a conception of God, but the religion of Islam is a direct revelation, and not a product of a philosophical genius. Mohammed was only a prophet. Everything in the Quran is a Divine Revelation (*tanzil*) that is, something 'sent down' (Surah 53:4). Mohammed did not write the Quran. After all, he was an *Ummi* (unlettered, stark illiterate, Surah 7:158). His childhood was marked with abject poverty, and so possibly he did not go to school. How then could he possibly have written a book — such a wonderful book? The Quran descended from heaven, and the original copy is still on the 'Preserved Tablet' or 'Mother of the Book' (*Umul al kitab*) in Paradise, and has been there even before the creation of the world! (Surah 6:92; 3:7; 43:3-4). And because of this, nothing in the book must be questioned.

The Western mind may find all of this indigestible and unbelievable. But they are not idle claims! Take them away, and there would be nothing called Islam.

They are what several hundred million Muslims believe, and they are the beliefs on which we have to base our study from the outset, at least before we can (ever) venture into re-examining them later.

The Allah we have in the Quran is therefore a revealed Allah and not just a conception (aql) emanating from Muslims' heads. Moreover, it is not only the Christians that say Allah is not "the God and Father of our Lord Jesus Christ". Whoever Allah is or is not, as we shall show in this book, is a revelation of the Quran rather than of Christians' claims.

The God in the Bible is not a description either. He revealed Himself to Abram, Jacob, Moses, the Prophets, and came down to manifest Himself physically in the Person of Jesus of Nazareth. Jesus said: *"he that hath seen me hath seen the Father;"* (John 14:9). Christians and the Jews did not conceive of the God in the Bible. God revealed Himself: His nature, His Name, His glory, His law, His judgment, His love, His holiness. Take away these revelations, and there would be nothing called Judaism or Christianity.

Today, Christians know God as He is in the Bible and in their lives. In the same vein, Allah is known to Muslims as he is in the Quran, and as he manifests himself in their lives. It is these revelations and manifestations (not descriptions) that determine the Islamic ethos and Christian ethics. Therefore, the problem before us is not that of different and conflicting descriptions of the Divine, but of revelations. And since these revelations are contained in the two books, the Quran and the Bible, they shall form the basis merely of identifying who Allah is.

In this work, we intend to explain the Quran as it is, by itself, with all its claims, taking Allah, the major character and comparing him with the character of the Christian God. We need to have our minds open in this venture. We need not be afraid

14

of being 'disturbed' with the facts. Such 'disturbances' are necessary. We would probably need permission from Muslims to quote from the Quran. Many Muslims resent a non-Muslim quoting from their sacred book for fear of an un-Islamic interpretation. But if the Quran contains clear facts and if it is the Word of God for the salvation of mankind, mankind must be free to read it and refer to it in a religious discourse. In the Bible, God allows even Satan(!) to quote from His Word (Matthew 4:5-7). But in quoting from the Quran, we may not agree with Al-A'shari that the Quran should be accepted *bi-la kayf* i.e. 'without asking questions'. As students, we beg for permission to reject this Islamic concept of "Ta abbudi" — that the Quran must "be accepted without criticism" As we proceed in the study of the Quran, we will have to ask certain questions. And the first question we wish to ask is:

Who Wrote The Quran?

We have already said something about the authorship of the Quran and will still discuss it in a later chapter. But the issue may need a further push. The general assumption we make here will determine how we can treat the issue before us. Generally, most Muslims believe that the Quran, their sacred book, came down from heaven and was given to Mohammed as a book or sheets in stages. The book itself claims in many verses that it was actually "sent down" from Allah (Surah 3:3; Surah 4:105; Surah 4:113; Surah 31:21; Surah 42:17; Surah 76:23). But if we are to take the Quran itself to determine its authorship from its claims, we cannot come out with a definite answer. For example, Surah 26:192-194 and Surah 16:102 say Mohammed received the Quran from "the Holy Spirit". But in Surah 53:2-18 and Surah 81:19-24, we read that it was the "one Mighty

15

in Power" himself that personally delivered the inspiration to Mohammed, and that Mohammed saw him. Elsewhere we read again that it was the angel Gabriel who brought the Quran down to Mohammed's heart by Allah's will (Surah 2:97). Again in Surah 15:8, we are made to know that it wasn't really Allah himself or Gabriel or the Holy Spirit, but actually "angels" (plural). If you are a Muslim and you are confused at this juncture, you have reasons enough to be so.

Some enlightened Muslims believe rather that it would be more reasonable to regard it as the written form of the verbal message given to Mohammed, and so a revelation. Reading through the comments of most Islamic scholars who translated the Quran, one easily sees that apart from their stereotypical romanticism, they too are not sure of the authorship of the book. All they can say is that it is the book of Allah.

A careful student who reads it either in the Arabic or in translations will see that apart from direct quotes from reported events, while some parts of the narratives are in the first person plural, some are in the third person and then first person singular, and so on. There are places where Allah is being addressed by the writer. The writer seems to forget he should maintain the narrative as coming from Allah and suddenly changes the narrative. For example, when the speaker/writer says: "For me, I have been commanded to serve the Lord in this city... and I am commanded to be of those who bow in Islam to God's will" (Surah 27:91), one may begin to wonder who is speaking — Allah or a writer? How could these statements have existed in a book in heaven before creation?

Some historians have attempted to prove that the Quran was not written by Mohammed nor even

16

during his life time. They say Mohammed was in fact illiterate. According to them, the book we call the Quran today is a product of some zealots of Islam under the supervision of a caliph, who, after the death of their master felt they must have a sacred book just as Christians and Jews have for their religion; and so they tried to recollect what their leader was preaching before his death. Part of it is said to be from the parchment written and kept before the death of the prophet. According to the Hadith, some of the fragments were collected from 'tablets of stone, ribs of palm branches, camels' shoulder-blades and ribs, pieces of board, and the breasts of men' (that is from men's memory).[2] The first attempt of compilation is said to have been made by Mohammed's daughter, Fatimah, who had to contest some of the facts with some of her father's followers since different versions were being recited by the people. Mohammed's wife, Hafsa, also helped in the compilation. The final work, however, is credited to Zaid ibn Thabit, whom some believe was merely the editor.

Because of the predominant use of both the first person plural and singular narratives, we want to make our first major assumption, and that is: there was a being from whom Mohammed was receiving his messages, and this being is called 'Allah' in Arabic, and even if the book were written by his followers after his death, they would have been able to remember some of the words flowing out from Mohammed when he was being inspired to recite the Quran.

This assumption is necessary because it helps us to establish our logic. If we accept the Quran as

2 for example see Mishkat al Masabih, Sh. M. Ashraf, Lahore (1990) p.469. Also Bukhari Vol. 9 No. 301.

divinely inspired by some Being, we should not be afraid to identify the Being. If we say from the outset that there was no supernatural being speaking to Mohammed or at least giving him the inspiration to say what he was quoted as saying, we would have no choice other than to dismiss the whole of the Quran and regard Mohammed as one of the most successful liars and deceivers the world has ever seen. This is because throughout the pages of the Quran, Allah is quoted exhaustively as one speaking, even in the first person plural, signifying a dignified or honorific Personality or deity.

So, we accept that there was an Allah talking to Mohammed or inspiring him. The issue we are faced with, basically, is whether or not the Allah from whose angel Mohammed was receiving his messages is the same as the Jehovah of the Bible.

We do not want to impose an opinion. We believe that in this book there are sufficient facts to enable you to draw your own conclusion. But, it is important for the Muslim reader to be very honest with himself and read the book through because this is a serious matter that has eternal consequences for the soul.

CHAPTER TWO

Allah And Violence

ONE thing we have to bear in mind is that Islam is spiritual, and a mere academic exercise in discussion of it will lead us nowhere. For example, it is easy for those who only hear or read about the violence and mysticism in Islam to explain away the religion only on exegetical levels. Violence in Islam is real and it is spiritual. No doubt, this is a very offensive area, but it is a fact all the same. And no matter how trenchant this may be, we know there are many honest Muslims who are ready to face and re-examine the facts and apply reason and not just get flared up emotionally.

Muslims And Christians, Must They Be Enemies?

Religious matters are perhaps the most complex issues in the world. In a speech on the need for peaceful co-existence of Muslims and Christians in the world, and particularly, in Nigeria, General Ibrahim Babangida a former President of Nigeria said:

"It may be a theological question whether God reveals himself or he reveals religion through his messenger, his prophet or his son. Irrespective of the position one takes on this issue, one should be reasonable enough to know that God, like the father of any household, can never be satisfied with members of the family who quarrel, fight, undermine and sometimes kill one another in his name."[1]

The pity is that many of us are indeed conscious of what God is supposed to be, yet personally we may be serving a wrong god with all sincerity. Why, because we may have found ourselves in a system

1 *New Nigerian*, October 19, 1988 p.3

and find it difficult to leave. Many of us do not see the need to leave a religious system because we may still be ignorant of the nature of the deception we have fallen into. If we can patiently journey together through this book, we may have to think again and reassess whatever it is we believe at present.

We believe that the pronouncement of General Babangida was made from an honest mind: "God can never be satisfied with quarrelling, fighting, undermining, killing in his name." That is true. But which God? Is it the common God, or Allah, the God of Mohammed? Or are they the same? That is the real 'theological question', and we need to discuss it.

We may need to link this question with a later event in Nigeria three years after this comment. In October 1991, German evangelist, Reinhard Bonnke, went to the city of Kano to preach. In their protest against the programme, the Muslims in Kano invited their fellow Jihâdists from Katsina State and embarked upon a riot that led to the slaughter of several Christians and Southern Nigerians in Kano. The Southerners felt that violence was not the monopoly of a particular people, and so took up arms against the Muslims until the latter were forced to ask for a ceasefire. Former President Babangida was on a visit outside the country then and had to rush back home. At the Airport in Lagos, he sympathized with the victims of the riot urging the nation to 'see the tragedy as a realisation of what God has ordained': "We continue to pray for the victims as good religious people in the country with the sense that it has been ordained by God that these things will happen."

Some observers had to ask: 'Why did he have to rush home from Zimbabwe to come and stop what 'God has ordained'? We too had to ask ourselves: Who is this 'God' that has been ordaining the killing of Christians in Nigeria all these years? Who is this 'God' that does not want the gospel of peace to be preached but has always been after the necks of 'the good religious people in the country'?

The other 'theological question' General Babangida raised in his statement of 1988 is the definition of 'the family' and 'the household'. General Babangida is a Muslim. And we need to point out that according to the Islamic thought, there are two distinct households in the world: the Dar ul-Islam ("household of Islam"), and Dar ul-Harb ("household of non-Islam or war"). Because they are two distinct households, they surely don't have the same father. And because Christians are non Muslims, they naturally belong to the latter household, the Dar ul-Harb.

So, when Babangida says 'the family', or 'the household', one wonders whether he is referring to the different sects in Islam, or to Christians and Muslims? Can he prove to Muslims that they are in the same family or household with Christians? Does the Quran say so? Does the Hadith say so? When a Muslim kills a Christian, is he killing 'one another' or he is only getting rid of a kaferi (infidel)? All these questions must be answered from the Quran itself and the Hadith and not from mere modern religious opinions.

In a seminar paper presented at the National Association for Religious and Ethnic Tolerance (NARETO) Conference in Lagos in August 1992, General Ibrahim Babangida said, "Islam has a full-fledged philosophy of religious tolerance and peaceful co-existence." We have studied the Quran from cover to cover again and again; we have also read a number of the Hadiths. We have not yet seen such a philosophy. The only place any Muslim can confidently point to in the Quran is Surah 2:256 which says in part, "Let there be no compulsion in religion". But we all know this statement was made at the early stage of Mohammed's mission, when he was just settling down in Yathrib (Medina). Such an attitude was necessary in order to get the co-operation of the Jewish tribes and Christians who were in the majority in Yathrib. Mohammed said he believed in all the Jewish prophets, and that he had not brought any new religion but the very things that the old prophets of Israel had preached. At that time, he did not have enough people to wage any war. When, however, he had raised enough military manpower, he began to launch out against those he suspected did not believe in his religion. Speaking as an oracle of Allah, Mohammed commanded that all those who opposed his message be killed or they should be nailed on a tree or their hands and legs be cut off, or they be driven out of the land. (Surah 5.36).

In Surah 47:4, Muslims are commanded by Allah to smite the necks of all those who do not accept the teachings of Islam until they are thoroughly subdued, and according to verse 7, they would be helping Allah by so doing. Others could be arrested and released only after paying a ransom. Surah 2:190-191, Surah 9:19-22, 29, 41 and several others, command true Muslims to fight those who oppose them or do not believe in the message of Islam: "So, when you meet (in fight — Jihâd in Allah's Cause), those who disbelieve smite at their necks till when you have killed and wounded many of them, then bind a bond firmly (on them, i.e. take them as captives)." (Surah 47:4 Al Hilali).

It is important to stress again that much of our discussion on Islam is not from Western historians but from the Quran and Islamic traditions called the Hadith and from present experiences in many parts of the world. We advise the reader to check

22

these references because most Muslims are wont to accuse any non-Muslim writer of quoting the Quran out of context.

We wish to say, however, that even though there were many killings done by Muslims when the religion came to Yathrib, we can say authoritatively that not all Muslims were intending initially to fight their fellow Meccan kinsmen or to loot their caravans in order to spread a religion. In Surah 4:74-80, many Arab Muslims protested Mohammed's call for *Jihâd* (Muslim holy war). They protested, "Our Lord! Why hast thou ordered us to fight?". But Mohammed convinced them that his command was directly from Allah.

The Quran says *Jihâd* is, in fact, not just a religious duty but a commerce, a business! (Surah 61:10-13). The Quran only promises spiritual rewards, but in the Hadith[2], *Jihâd* is said to be "the best method of earning (blessings) both spiritual and temporal. If victory is won, there is enormous booty of a country, which cannot be equalled to any other source of income. If there is defeat or death, there is everlasting paradise". So, we conclude that *Jihâd* is NOT extremism, but normal in Islam.

A Christian Missionary once asked a Muslim man, "What if your son became a Christian? What would you do? 'I'd cut his throat,' the Muslim said".[3]

Such may not be the case in most families. But it is very costly for anyone to be converted to the Christian faith from an Islamic family. With our experience of working among Muslims in many parts of the world, we can say that the greatest hindrance

---

2 *Mishkat Masabih* Vol II, Page 253, cited in Gerhard Nehls, A guide to Muslim Evangelism, Life Challenge, Nairobi p.4

3 Sumrall, Lester: *Where was God when Pagan Religions Began?* Thomas Nelson, Nashville (1980) p138

to a Muslim's decision to follow Christ is FEAR — fear of what other Muslims would do to him or her. Even when a Muslim is convicted of his sins, or is convinced of the truth of the Christian faith, he still fears the implications of conversion. Most former Muslims who are Christians today have stories to tell in this regard. Many of them are disowned. We have known of a specific case of parents poisoning their daughter for denouncing Islam and becoming a Christian. Even at the time of this editing, we have a case of a lady whose Muslim parents and relatives are threatening her to renounce her new faith in Christ and re-embrace Islam or face the consequences. A letter from Sokoto in Nigeria says: "A man here got converted ... and since he still lived in the family house, his parents (as usual here) parked all his personal belongings and set fire to them while he was away at his job".

We must never imagine that such Muslims are being unnecessarily wicked. They are simply being faithful to their religion. The fact is never hidden as to the attitude a good Muslim should have towards Christians and Jews. In fact, much of the incitement to violence and war in the whole of the Quran is directed against the Jews and Christians who rejected what they felt to be the strange god Mohammed was trying to preach. It wasn't long before pagan Arabians submitted to Islam since Allah was one of the several gods of the people. But Jews and Christians were recalcitrant, feeling they had a better God. They were slow and reluctant to accept one of the pantheons of Arabia. They probably remembered the Scripture that *"ALL the gods of the people* (in whatever guise) *are idols:"* (1 Chronicles 16:26). In plain terms, therefore, Mohammed or Allah (or whoever is speaking in the Quran) says:

"O you who believe! Take not the Jews and the Christians as 'Auliyâ' (friends, protectors, helpers etc.), they are but 'Auliyâ' to one another. And if any amongst you takes them as 'Auliyâ' then surely he is one of them. Verily, Allah guides not those people who are the Zâlimûn (polytheists and wrongdoers and unjust)" (Surah 5:51 Al Hilali. Verse 54, Yusuf Ali).

In other words, any Muslim who becomes a Christian or even befriends a Christian leaves the leadership and control of Allah.

So, all Islamic leaders who come to British and American Church leaders for inter-faith co-operation are either defying the instructions of Allah or they have a hidden agenda. The Islam of the 7th century A.D. is the same today, probably under new guises as the situation demands. It is the same tactic of "No compulsion in religion" that Mohammed first adapted to Christians and Jews, that Muslims are using in the Western world today. Migrate to Christian areas because they are tolerant. Pretend to be peaceful, friendly and hospitable; begin to clamour for religious, political and social rights and privileges that you will not allow to Christians in an Islamic country; breed fast there and settle down; there should be no Christian activities in your community; you may speak or write to discredit their religion, but they must not talk about Islam; begin to expand your community; Christian activities should be restricted in all the places you expand to; the moment you have enough military might against these 'disbelievers', these trinitarian kaferis, go ahead and eliminate them or suppress them as much as you can, and be in control. Where immediate invasion is not possible, that has always been the policy.

There are so many incitements against Christians and non-Muslims running through the pages of the Quran that we find it hard to believe that anybody can

25

be a real practising Muslim now or then and not hate Christians. It is impossible. Any Muslim who is not violent (secretly or openly) is hardly a real Muslim, at least not in the Quranic sense. It means he has not got the spirit of Islam. A typical practising Muslim must be violent, especially if he expects to get any reward in the Muslim heaven: "Let those who fight in the way of Allah who sell the life of this world for the other. Whoso fighteth in the way of Allah, be he slain or be he victorious, on him We shall bestow a vast reward...Hast thou not seen those unto whom it was said: Withhold your hands, establish worship and pay the poor-due, but when fighting was prescribed for them behold! a party of them fear mankind even as their fear of Allah or with greater fear," (Surah 4:74, 77 Pickthall).

If words have meaning, then we can confidently say from the quotation above that submission to Allah (Islam) is not just in prayers and zakat as some would want us to believe, but in obedience to the order for killing in order to spread Islam. That is the Islam of Mohammed. We have an overwhelming monument of evidence from both the Quran and the Hadith to prove our claims here. For want of space, we can give only a few more examples. In the Hadith[4] the mother of Haritha was assured by Mohammed that Haritha had attained the highest garden in paradise because he had died in battle. In the same Hadith Mohammed also said:

"No warlike party or body of troops will go out to fight, gain booty and return safe without getting beforehand two-thirds of their rewards in full".

"He who dies without having fought, or having felt it to be his duty will die guilty of a kind of hypocrisy".

---

4 Mishkat al Masabih Sh. M. Ashraf (1990) pp.147, 721, 810, 811, 1130.

"There is no emigration after the Conquest, but only *Jihâd* and some good intention; so when you are summoned to fight, go forth".

"The last hour will not come before the Muslims fight the Jews and the Muslims kill them".

"Three people are all in God's safekeeping: a man who goes out to fight in God's path, who is in God's safekeeping till He takes his soul and brings him to paradise, or sends him home with the reward or booty he has obtained...".

Abu Dharr said he asked the Prophet what action was most excellent, and he replied, "Faith in God and *Jihâd* (fighting) in His path".

Those Liberal Muslim scholars who are getting embarrassed with the amount of terrorism being perpetrated in the world today by Muslims try to explain *Jihâd* away, saying physical fighting was never part of the 'original' Islam, and that this was a misinterpretation of Allah's injunction by some fanatical Muslims of this generation. In the light of the above clear instructions in both the Quran and the Hadith, such scholars have no case.

As for many Westerners who are bothered about Islamic terrorism in the world today, it is because they are so engrossed with technology that they forget history. Dr Jane Smith of Harvard University has clearly shown in a dissertation that even the term "Islam" did not originally mean "submission". Also in *The Spiritual Background of Islam*, Middle East scholar Dr M. Bravmann reveals that the term 'Islam' did not originally mean Mohammed's religion or that of any Jewish patriarchal religion as claimed by Muslims. According to Dr Bravmann, the word "Islam" was "a secular concept denoting a sublime virtue in the eyes of the primitive Arab; defiance of death, heroism; to die in battle". The term denoted bravery in battle. It did not mean peace or submission.

Marshal Hodgson reminds us that the English word "assassin" is purely of Arabic origin. It was originally "Hashshashin", (or assassinus in Latin) meaning 'smokers of hashish'. It referred to a certain sect of Muslims in the 11th–13th centuries who took hashish (hemp) to receive enough energy to fight for Allah by killing non-Muslims.

In this Chapter, we intend to show that Islam, past or present, is not what many people say it is. Mohammed's wealthy wife, Khadija bint Khuwaylid, and his powerful uncle, Abu Talib, both of whom Meccans had been afraid of, died in the same year — in fact, within thirty days of each other. This was a big blow to Mohammed. He felt insecure and this was the reason why he had to flee to Taif and later to Yathrib (Medina). Those who had fled with him soon settled down. The people of Yathrib had welcomed them and had been generous to them. But this could not continue forever.

Life soon became difficult for these settlers economically, and they had to survive. Mohammed therefore felt that he had to take revenge on the Meccan merchants for the hostility he had suffered in Mecca. But because of their ethnic affiliation, as we have noted earlier, many of the Muslims did not see why they should attack and loot their own tribesmen in order to survive or because of a religion. But a revelation came to Mohammed from Allah to justify this first mobilisation for *Jihâd*. And so, in Surah 2:216, we read, "*Jihâd* (Islamic holy war) is ordained for you (Muslims) though you dislike it, and it may be that you dislike a thing which is good for you and that you like a thing which is bad for you. Allah knows but you do not know." (Al Hilali).

With this revelation, Muslims set out on their first *Jihâd* and defeated these Meccans and looted them. The booty carried from the Meccans served as an encouragement for Muslims for further *Jihâd*s. The Meccans in retaliation, mobilised about 1,000 fighters against Mohammed. With only about 300 people, the Muslims tactically defeated the Meccans. This was the battle of BaDr These victories seemed to prove that Allah was supporting them, and that Mohammed was truly sent.

Later, covenants were made between Mohammed and the Meccans not to fight for a certain number of years. All these covenants were cancelled by Mohammed together with those made with the Jews in Yathrib. Let us hear this in the words of Shaykh (Sheikh) Abdullah bin Muhammad bin Hamid of the Sacred Mosque of Mecca:

"Then Allah revealed in Surah Bara'at (Repentance, IX) the order to discard (all) obligations (covenants), etc, and commanded the Muslims to fight all the pagans as well as against the people of the Scriptures (Jews and Christians) if they do not embrace Islam, till they pay the Jizya (A tax levied on those who do not embrace Islam..) Muslims were not permitted to abandon 'the fighting' against them (pagans, Jews and Christians) and to reconcile with them and to suspend hostilities against them for an unlimited period while they are strong and have the possibility of fighting against them." Here, the reason for killing Christians and Jews is clear: '**if they do not** embrace Islam'. This is contrary to what some modern Muslim revisionists claim. *Jihâd* against Christians was NOT defensive but offensive, and we need to emphasise this (Surah 9:29, 123).

Shaykh bin Hamid continues: "So at first, 'the fighting' was FORBIDDEN, then it was PERMITTED, and after that it was made OBLIGATORY — Allah made 'the fighting' (*Jihâd*) obligatory for Muslims and gave importance to the subject matter of *Jihâd* in ALL the Surahs which were revealed (at Medina) as it is in Allah's statement: 'March forth whether you are light (being healthy, young and wealthy) or heavy (being ill, old and poor) and strive hard with your wealth and your lives in the cause of Allah. That is better for you if you (but) knew'" (Surah 9:41).

Many Muslims do not like reading about the violence in Islam as they believe this is a misrepresentation. But can they ignore their history? Mohammed not only commanded wars, but was also involved in person. During his life time, alone, sixty-six battles were fought by his army, of which he personally led twenty-seven. It was on a battle ground (Battle of Uhud, 625 A.D.) that Mohammed broke one of his teeth. Some traditions say two front teeth. Some say that the wars were political rather than religious. From the quotations above, we know that such a claim has no foundation. In any case, Islam draws no distinction between religion and politics.

A number of writers who criticise Islam today have lost their freedom; some even losing their lives in Islamic countries. Egyptian writer, Farag Fouda, was murdered early in 1992 by Muslims for criticising Islamic militancy. The Speaker of that country's Parliament was also assassinated in 1990 for his anti-Islamic stance, and the militant Muslims claimed responsibility. Muslims never like anybody going into the real history of their religion. But these are no strange things. Among the first blood shed by Mohammed's followers in Medina was that of a poetess, Asma, daughter of Merwan and wife of Yazid bin Zaid. According to Ibn Ishaq in his monumental work *Suraht'l Rasul*, translated by Ibn Hisham as *The Life of the Prophet*, Mrs. Asma Yazid had composed and popularized some poems to ridicule the people of Medina for following a man who has slain 49 of his own tribesmen at Badr and looted their caravan in order to establish a religion. This woman was stabbed on her bed. The assignment was carried out by 'Umayr ibn 'Awf. In the words of Muslim scholar Muhammad Haykal, "'Umayr ibn Awf attacked her during the night while she was surrounded by her children, one of whom she was nursing. 'Umayr was weak of sight and had to grope for her. After removing the child from his victim, he killed her; he then proceeded to the Prophet and informed him of what he had done."[5] He received a commendation for having done a good job for Allah. About three other poets who could not be silent had their necks face the sharp edge of the Islamic sword and soon lost their heads. One of them was Abu 'AFak.

Another poet (and soldier), Abbas, was to face a similar judgment. It was after the Battle of Honain. The problem arose as to the way Mohammed shared the booty. Abbas, said to be a 'lukewarm convert', grumbled about the Apostle's arithmetic of sharing the booty, and registered his complaint in a few verses. "The Apostle overheard him and said with a smile, 'Take that man from here and cut out his tongue'." [6]

Even though Ayatollah Khomeini belonged to the Shiite sect of Islam, he was generally regarded as an exemplary Muslim of our time. Following the foot-steps of the prophet of Allah in establishing an Islamic state, Khomeini slaughtered more people during the first few years of his reign than were killed during all the years of his predecessor, Shah Muhammad Reza Pahlavi. After all the massacres of non-Muslims in Persia (present Iran), Khomeini said: "In Persia no people have been killed so far — only beasts!"

5 Haykal, M. *The Life of Mohammed.* Lagos: Islamic Publications Bureau (1982)

6 Khan, M. Ebrahim. *Anecdotes from Islam,* Sh. Muhammad Ashraf, Lahore (1960) p.20

On another occasion, this servant of Allah said: "The purest joy in Islam is to kill and be killed for Allah."[7] Early in 1984, Ayatollah Khomeini was quoted as saying: "In order to achieve the victory of Islam in the world, we need to provoke repeated crises, restore value to the idea of death and martyr dom. If Iran has to vanish, that is not important. The important thing is to engulf the world in crises".[8] From our studies of the Quran so far, was Khomeini sounding un-quranic or un-allahic? Was he being fanatical?

Serious Muslims are morbidly worried about the way Christianity is growing today. The South African Muslim *Jihâd*ist, Ahmed Deedat, is concerned that: "Kuwait (a Muslim country) had just one Arab Christian family about fifty years ago. Today there are thirty-five churches in that little country".[9] He is obsessed that in the Muslim country of Indonesia, there are 6,000 full-time foreign Christian missionaries "harassing" non-Christians. He decries the way Christianity is growing, especially in Africa, and therefore reminds Muslims to go back to the original Islam given by Allah in the Quran: "Our armour, sword and shield in this battle of Faiths are in the Koran, we have been chanting it for centuries... now we must bring them forth into the battlefield".[10]

What are the "armour, sword and shield in this battle of faiths"?

They are physical armour, physical swords and all available modern weapons of warfare. Shaykh

---

7 Lamb, David: *The Arabs*, Random House, New York (1987) p287

8 *Le Point Magazine*, No. 599, 12 March, 1984, pp 89,91

9 Deedat, Ahmed, *What is his Name?* Islamic Propagation Centre, Durban, (1986) p.13

10 Deedat, A. op cit. p.14

Abdullah bin Muhammad bin Hamid, quoted earlier, explains:

"To get ready (for *Jihâd*) includes various kinds of preparations and weapons. Tanks, missiles, artillery, aeroplanes, naval ships etc, and the training of the soldiers in these instruments of war are all included under the word 'force', (to include land force, navy and air-force)". In a way, Khomeini, Deedat, and other real Muslims are right. How can Islam spread otherwise? What message of salvation have they to offer convincingly to a sinning world than to repeat 'la-illaha il allah' a million times? Is the modern man not getting sick of this chanting? Perhaps they should use their oil money to build many multi-million dollar mosques all over the world to give an impression that Islam is spreading everywhere. The policy is, 'let there be mosques everywhere' — even if there are no people to occupy them. Within a period of only five years (1985-1990), Muslims erected 5,002 mosques in Ethiopia alone. In 1945, only one mosque was to be found in the whole of England. In 1990 over 1,000 mosques are scattered all over the country. In 1974, there was only one mosque in France. Today, more than 1,700 have been built there.

Even though Muslims claim that they are serving the same God as Christians, yet in reality, they see Christianity as the greatest threat to the incursion of Islam in any land. Despite the apostasy in the Western world, Christianity is still growing at an alarming rate, and Muslims are aware of this. Hundreds of thousands of converts are being made into the Christian faith every year in the free world, and ironically, millions in Communist China. A 1988 survey by Newsweek magazine shows Latin Americans coming to Christ en masse everyday. How can Christian activities be countered by Muslims?

Apart from proliferating mosques, one alternative, especially in Africa, is to entice nominal Christian girls with money, stockfish, job, and marry them, and then convert them to Islam. Muslim youths who succeed in marrying Christian girls are rewarded. Huge sums of money are offered to people to convert them to Islam. The targets for conversion are those with some 'Christian' background — Jehovah Witnesses and Catholics or some other nominal Christians. A report from a friend in Tanzania says, "It's common knowledge in our area that you can gain a TSH 25,000/- reward for winning over a Christian to become a Muslim, and TSH 100,000/- if you succeed in converting a pastor or priest to Islam."

An alternative for multiplying is to have several wives and produce more Muslim children to overpopulate the world and then claim the Muslim population to be in the hundreds of millions. According to a U.N. report, the world population in the '90s is growing at the rate of three babies per second (and Muslims have a fair share of this). While an American or European will have one wife and one or two children, Muslims world-wide reproduce themselves in great numbers every year. It is estimated that the Islamic world produces 25 million babies annually. That is a way of Islamising the world! Biological evangelisation! And this must never be sneered at. Muslims are confident that with liberal immigration laws in the U.S.A., Europe and the U.K., in particular, they will soon be in the majority and a strong force to be reckoned with, politically.

Another possibility is to woo poor nations with oil money and initiate them into the Organization of Islamic Conferences (O.I.C.). It is a simple principle: he that controls your stomach controls your life. Even in the West, the huge investment of Arab petro-dollars is gradually enslaving us.

But these alternatives are not bringing the best results. Christianity is spreading everywhere. Muslim youths are turning from what some of them regard as an 'empty monotonous religiosity' and opting for something more real and vivacious in Christianity. Many young Muslim ladies are now renouncing their Islamic names. Many of them consider their marital role in Islam and opt for Christianity. Some Imams and great alhajis and alhajas are declaring Jesus as Lord.

Nigerian Christians are facing tense opposition from Islam now because of the phenomenal growth of the Gospel in that country, and the rate at which Muslims are getting converted to the Christian faith. The Church in Nigeria is an aggressively praying Church and this has been a key factor behind the present success of mission and evangelistic works in that country. The devil is not unaware of this, and he can't simply sit down and do nothing. It is not uncommon in Northern Nigeria to hear of "Reverend Ahmed Abdkadir" or "Pastor Sanni Abubakar Yusuf". Nothing can be more annoying to Islamic leaders than this.

To ensure the victory of Islam, therefore, something drastic has to be done. How did the religion spread in its early stage? Genuine Muslims must return to the effective Islam of Mohammed. Who is a real Muslim? "It is only those who believe not in Allah and the Last Day and whose hearts are in doubt that ask your leave (to be exempted from *Jihâd*)." (Surah 9:45 Al Hilali). This means that claiming to be a real Muslim and refusing to engage in physical fighting is apostasy.

In the Preface to *The Call of Jihâd*, Mallam M. Salih exclaims: "What a hypocrite is a man who regards the *Jihâd* as an antiquated duty in Islam."

As a matter of fact, there are no intolerant or fanatical extremes of Islam. All violent acts and vandalism that may be, are only normal to the religion.

35

The so-called fanatical Muslims are the real Muslims. Yes, the Maitatsinis, the Zalla, the Muslim youth organizations and their sponsors, al-Jihâd groups in Lebanon, al-Mujahideens of Iran, the Muslim Brotherhood in Egypt and some other countries, the Muslim Students Society (MSS), the Jamat'ul Nasril Islamiyya (JNI), etc. — these are the Genuine Muslims. They must establish the kingdom of God on earth.

Their understanding of the kingdom of God is radically different from that of the Bible. The Bible says 'the meek shall inherit the earth'. Christ Himself said, *'Blessed are the meek, for they shall inherit the earth.'* Islam says no, you cannot be meek and inherit the earth; the believer must rise up now and overthrow the government and be in control. The Quran says, "might belongeth to Allah and to His messenger and the believers;" (Surah 63:8 Pickthall). It is therefore necessary for the Genuine Muslim to cause *fitna* (anarchy, trouble) until a pure kingdom of Allah is established in a land. That was the spirit of the Revolution that brought Khomeini to power; it is the spirit driving the Muslim Brotherhood in Egypt and the Alawites in Syria. It is the Islam of Mohammed and the world must no longer misunderstand their violent actions. When Muslims destroyed Churches and killed Christians in Kaduna State, Nigeria, in 1987, a panel was set up by the government to investigate the issue. All parties involved in the incident were asked to submit memoranda to the panel. In Section 4, subsection (C) of its own memorandum, the Jama'atu Nasril Islamiyya (JNI) said: "It is very often found that people who are ignorant of Islam and Muslims have wrong impressions of the Muslims. Such ignorant Christians give Muslims all sorts of bad names such as 'fundamentalists', 'fanatics,' etc as a quality for any faithful Muslims who believe in living according to Islamic injunctions. Muslims who are not serious about their religion are regarded as progressive. If the Christians knew Islam well, they would not waste their time trying to stand in their way as they would realize that ... nothing could stand in the way of the real faithful Muslims."

We can understand the irony and the undertone here. These are the genuine Muslims. The fact is that it is we Christians that have been ignorant of what really faithful Muslims are supposed to be, and we should be really sorry for such ignorance. It has become a tradition for most leaders in Africa and in many parts of the world during Muslim festival periods to send messages to Muslims to follow the example of the prophet Mohammed and obey Allah, and then have religious tolerance. Either these leaders are yet to know what Islam is, or they are just trying to say something to make news during every Sallah period. It is utterly impossible to follow Mohammed's example in the Hadiths and obey his Allah in the Quran and then be peaceful, tolerant and submissive to a government that is not entirely Islamic.

Even in a country like Egypt where all the key leaders are Muslims, there will still be unrest among Muslims until a pure Islamic government is established and imposed on all other people in the land. So long as Coptic Christians remain in the land and their churches are still visible, Muslims will never rest. In September 1981, the Muslims went on an onslaught against the Copts and left 50 dead. Because of this, the then President, Anwar Sadat, ordered a wave of arrests and trials of fundamentalists. A month later, an underground Islamic group assassinated him.

Hosni Mubarak, who is trying to present himself as a strict upholder of Islamic values in order to pacify the Jihâdists, is soon discovering the futility of such thinking. The militants are trying to destroy his rule and establish a pure Islamic rule in the land. To this end, tourism, the mainstay of the Egyptian economy, is being disrupted. This is being done by killing Western tourists visiting the historical monuments in Upper Egypt. In mid-October 1992, a British tourist was killed with a machine gun. The *Middle East* magazine reported that the Islamic militants "opened fire on a Nile cruise ship carrying 140 German tourists ... And on Oct. 25, three Russian tourists were stabbed in the Mediterranean town of Port Said".

There is no President's message that can change a genuine Muslim in the area of violence and anger. What a Muslim needs is a spirito-surgical operation — an operation done by the Holy Spirit of God on the spirit or heart of man — a complete overhaul of the heart. It is a spiritual heart-transplant, a trans plantation of a new nature, a new gene. That is why it is known as a re–gene–ration. It is what Jesus simply calls being born again (John 3:3).

At Christmas and Easter times, our political leaders make their traditional messages to Christians to be peaceful. We thank them for such messages. But Christians do not need a politician or a uniformed man to tell them to be peaceful. We have enough pastors who can do that better under the anointing of God. It is not a speech by some press secretary that can make a Christian peaceful or holy, for our God teaches us not only to *"follow peace with all men,"* but also to *"turn the other cheek"* even in the face of provocation! *"But I say unto you which hear, Love your enemies, do good to them which hate you, Bless them that curse you, and pray for them which despitefully use you. And unto him that smiteth thee on the one cheek, offer also the other;"* (Luke 6:27-29).

That indeed sounds outlandish, but it is one of the teachings of our own Saviour. No religion can preach that. Jesus Himself demonstrated this by laying down His life so that those who believe in Him might have eternal life. He is our Shepherd and we are His sheep. And as sheep, we have no horns to fight, nor upper teeth to bite. God is the One that fights on our behalf. We do not need a politician to tell us that. It seems many of our leaders condone or even promote Islam and yet tell Muslims to be peaceful. Until a Muslim is born again, he can hardly be peaceful. To imagine a really peaceful and gentle Muslim is like imagining a weightless stone, a round square or an elastic glass. You can trust a Muslim to be a Muslim. As we have seen, in the Quran, Mohammed, quoting Allah, said: "Fight against those who believe not in Allah…and those who acknowledge not the religion of truth (i.e. Islam) among the people of the Scripture (Jews and Christians) until they pay the *Jizya*" (Surah 9:29 Al Hilali). In Surah 4:89, Allah commands that any person who leaves Islam or encourages others to do so, should be seized and slain. That is the main reason why Muslims are very much afraid of being converted to Christianity.

Now, if by believing and practising the gospel of Jesus Christ I become the enemy of Allah, who could this Allah be? Who is this Allah that is so offended by the gospel of Christ? Can he be the God of the Bible who singled out Jesus in the midst of the two greatest prophets of the Bible, and then marked Him out as *"This is my beloved Son: hear Him"* (Luke 9:35)? If by "hearing Him" we offend an Allah, don't we have good reasons to probe the identity of this Allah? "Send missionaries to Burundi, Zaire, Uganda…to combat the evil activities of Christian missionaries there," said Muammar Ghaddafi of Libya. "God wants you to fight in one rank and he who does not do this is outside Islam and God will not let him enter paradise... You must incite Muslims in Zaire and urge them to engage in *Jihâd* so that Mobutu may be toppled. He who kills this man will go to paradise".[11] Woe to the nation ruled by such a 'God'!

In a very prophetic utterance, Jesus said concerning Christians: *"the time cometh, that whosoever killeth you will think that he doeth God service. And these things will they do unto you, because they have not known the Father, nor me."* (John 16:2-3). This simply means that the Allah our killers claim to know as God may not be the real Father. And this is why we have to take the pains and patience to find out who this god of Islam is. A Muslim need not get upset by such a venture. It is necessary.

The Nigerian Experience

As Islam was practised by Mohammed, so it is today. No extremism. In fact, there is less carnage today than then. This is obviously because there are civil and criminal laws and orders that handicap any savage behaviour in the name of religion. Nigeria has seen practical Islam; and there are too many cases for us to cite. We shall recall only a few of the more recent ones. We remember the 1980 Maitatsine Islamic uproar in Kano during which 4,177 people were officially reported as slaughtered with property worth millions of dollars destroyed. Two years later, on October 30, 1982, eight big Churches were burnt in Kano. That same year the Muslims struck in Kaduna and 400 people were officially reported as killed. In October of the same year, members of the Muslim Students Society (MSS) struck in Sabon Gari in Kano and killed two people. Many of the killings were not just of Christians but also of the people of different sects in the same religion of Islam.

---

11 *Nigerian Sunday Punch*, 26 January, 1986

In 1984, Muslims in Yola and Jimeta went berserk and killed 700 including policemen, and 5,913 people were rendered homeless. They also besieged Gombe and more than 100 people were killed.[12]

On May 3, 1986, the Muslim students of the then University of Sokoto went on a rampage attacking other students with dangerous weapons. While these Muslim students were still boiling in Sokoto, their counterparts in Ibadan were setting fire to the sculpture of Jesus in the Chapel of the Resurrection at the University of Ibadan. The following year, March 6, 1987, at the College of Education, Kafanchan in Kaduna State, Muslims went on a rampage they expected would spread to the South. This engulfed Kafanchan itself, Kaduna and Zaria. Of all the 150 churches in Zaria alone, only one escaped being burnt down in three days of *Jihâd* in that town. Many Christians were slain in cold blood while some were burnt alive. Many houses belonging to Christians and cars with Christian stickers were burnt in those cities. This writer was in Kaduna and Zaria to see things for himself. The imme- diate cause of the riot: A female Muslim student of the college accused Reverend Abubakar Bako, a former Muslim, of 'misinterpreting' the Quran, in his preaching. No non-Muslim must quote from the Quran, even though a Muslim can quote from the Bible. For them, a person who is not a Muslim cannot understand what the Quran says on any issue.

During this crisis, the Chaplain of the Ahmadu Bello University, Kongo Campus, Dr Ben Oruma, the man whose ministry in the Chapel has helped in depopulating the Muslim students in the university, was one of their main targets of assassination. From his house, he was pursued for several miles. Then, finally, they got him, slashed his body with

12 *Times International*, Lagos 19th March 1984 p.6

knives; matcheted and clobbered him. "They thought that they had finished me," said Dr Oruma, "And as they were going, I faintly heard them chanting 'Allahu Akbar, Allahu Akbar'" i.e. Allah is greater, Allah is greater... that is, for handing over his enemy into their hands.

It would be impossible for this book to contain reports of all the atrocities perpetrated in Nigeria by Muslims since the Uthman Dan Fodio *Jihâd* in 1804. Yet such horrors must never be taken as extremism. One of the aims of this book is to show that violence in Islam is both a doctrine and a person. In Christianity, peace is also both a teaching to obey and a Person to possess. When one is possessed with any of these 'persons', one can't help but behave accordingly. Try to find a genuine committed Muslim who is peaceful and gentle, and you may soon discover that if you press a button in his life, his real nature will manifest. The seemingly most peaceful among them have proved this to us. But they have killed us only to embolden us. Our voice is louder at death than in life. Thousands of us have been slaughtered; but Muslims must never think they have succeeded in silencing us.

One thing must be clear, however, and Muslims in the West must take note. We are not going to wait for Islam to stifle us and enslave our free nations as they did in North Africa, and in many other places in the world where it has become an offence to openly confess the Christian faith or convert a person to Christianity. Muslims need to beware; our God will not forget centuries of repeated assaults by Muslims and He will bring every one to justice. We hope any responsible government will take a serious caution from here. As merciful as our God is, He never forgives anyone who does not acknowledge his sins and repent. Muslims have not repented and they must therefore not think they can continue in their savagery unchecked.

In 1991 and 1992 there were three more riots by Muslims in Katsina, Bauchi and Kano during which thousands lost their lives. In Bauchi, the immediate cause was the sale of roasted pork or suya by a Christian, in Tafawa Balewa, a Christian area, which a Muslim bought and allegedly ate. The meat seller was killed for 'tempting' the Muslim. Hundreds of souls from both sides died in the riots that followed.

In Kano, the Muslims were rioting to protest against a proposed Christian evangelistic programme by the German preacher, Reinhard Bonnke. Many unprintable atrocities were reported. Two members of the Nigerian publishers of this book went to Kano immediately after the riot. One of the stories making its rounds in the city then was that of a pregnant woman whom some Jihâdists reportedly dragged out of a hospital, slashed her womb with a dagger and flung out 'the infidel thing inside her'. A team of *The Nigerian Newswatch* magazine who went to cover the butchery wrote that it would be against decency to publish some of the pictures they took in Kano. It seems we easily forget history, and by that we can put our generation and our posterity in danger. This book is dedicated to an elder of the ECWA Church, Tundun Wada, in Kaduna, whom Muslims burnt to death together with his church during the 1987 riots. This church was rebuilt at the cost of N500,000. In May 1992 Muslims burnt the church again. There was a Christian play going on in the church that evening. A band of Muslims just came, surrounded it and set the church on fire, killing at least 20 people inside. The assistant secretary, Musa Bakut, was not there; but the Muslims went to look for him in his house and slaughtered him and his son, burnt his car and left his wife half dead. They decided not to finish her because they suddenly remembered that Allah says they should not kill women or little children. All this was during the Zango kataf Kaduna riots, which — we are repeatedly told — had nothing to do with religion.

The Philosophy Of Peace

We are aware there are as many opinions as there are people in the world. There are those who may sympathize with Christians for the damage being done to them by the Muslims, and yet believe that to probe the Muslim god would be extreme. For such people, a book such as this will be seen as offensive. They do not realise that *even the Bible* is offensive to Muslims. They believe Christians should remain silent or just simply complain in their rooms. A writer should respect others' religion and their feelings? He should be tolerant — that is to remain silent even though his very right to existence is taken away. He does allow peace to reign!

People with such opinions surely do not understand what peace means in Islam. There is a Jewish ballad that tells of a sardine swimming off the shores of Eilat. He meets a shark and humbly says the normal greeting, *shalom* or peace. To avoid any clash, the sardine gives up his tail, some fins, some scales but it seems all these avail nothing. Now, for a real and lasting peace, he surrenders everything. The shark nods in agreement and utters the word 'peace', opens his mouth and swallows the sardine whole. That is the peace, the lasting peace.

In government offices in Northern Nigeria, the Christian's fins, tail and scales have been chopped off by his Muslim boss. His schools (where the Muslim big man was also educated), as well as his hospitals, have been taken over and given Islamic names. But all this is not the lasting peace.

For Islam, peace or 'salaam' is not achieved until Islam has swallowed the nation. Peace means total eradication of enemies. It means subjugating, killing or swallowing all non-conformists. Nobody should therefore ever imagine 'giving peace a chance' in a nation with a significant number of Muslims.

As Richard Wurmbrand has said, Christians are not going to quarrel, but we are not going to allow anybody to swallow us either. "Children of God are too valuable a species; we have to survive... while we must loathe war, we also had to defeat Hitler, the lover of war."[13]

Late in 1989, key Muslim leaders from all over Africa gathered in Nigeria. One of the resolutions was to establish 'The Islam in Africa Organisation' (IAO). The IAO was founded, and Nigeria was made its 'permanent headquarters'. Members concluded: "We are ready to go any length to get Sharia established in this country whether we are alive or dead."[14]

Should Christians be silent so that we do not provoke a riot? Muslims do not need to be provoked. For them, it does not take two to fight. If they have to obey the injunctions of Allah in the Quran and follow Mohammed's examples and instructions in the Hadith, they do not have to be provoked. Genuine Muslims are always meditating on what next to do to 'convert' the enemies of Allah. For them, everybody must be judged by Sharia, the law of Allah.

Muslim leaders are now working very hard to engulf not only Africa but the Western world. Billions of petro-dollars are being spent to erect mosques in Britain, Europe, Australia and the United States. When the International Islamic Conference was held in Britain in 1976, Muslims

---

13 Wurmbrand, R. *A Hundred Meditations*, p.142
14 *Daily Sketch*, Ibadab, December 14, 1989, p. 8

determined and vowed, "If we can win London for Islam, it won't be hard to win the whole Western world."

Most English people do not even imagine the possibility of Muslims realising such an aspiration. But the progress Islam has made in Britain is great. Over 1000 mosques are already here. Because of our Christian heritage God's blessing has made the western nations relatively prosperous. Many Muslims, seeing the economic benefits, are fleeing to the West. But instead of us presenting the gospel to them, Muslims are being encouraged to establish mosques and madrassas and continue their religion here. We may think we are helping them; but we are not. Instead of these people settling down to begin a new and quiet life in the free world, they are now demanding an Islamic Parliament. Their clamour has been influencing the British Lawmakers in many areas especially concerning the status of Christianity and Islam in the land. They are also calling for laws in Britain to amputate the hands of thieves as is done in Islamic countries, making Sharia operative in the Western world. If Muslims are convinced that their god has to rule us in the free world, they should allow us to study that god and his manifestos and constitution thoroughly first; for the Bible says: *"Blessed is the nation whose God is the LORD."* If the Muslim god is the Allah of the Islamic strongholds of the world where one cannot speak of freedom or fundamental human rights; if he is the god of Kuwait where a woman cannot vote, or the god of Saudi where a woman must not drive a car, or the god of Iran where a wife has to get an 'exit permit' from her husband before coming out of the house; if he is the inspirer of Mohammed and the speaker in the Quran, we in the free world would need some time to study him first to determine whether or not we should allow him to rule our land.

The Western world, especially Britain, has an illusion of maintaining a standard of being fair to all, not wanting to annoy Muslims. The Australian Parliament is even trying to make a law against speaking anything against other people's religion. All this is hypocrisy because many things are said and written against biblical Christianity by the press all over the world, especially by Muslim writers, and nobody seems to object.

The aim of Islam is to engulf the world. As a matter of policy, Muslims do not want to be 'offended' or 'assaulted'; but they can go to any length to assault other religions, especially, Christianity. In Islamic countries, it is lawful for a Muslim to convert a Christian to Islam, but illegal, and in fact, a serious crime for a Christian to attempt to convert a Muslim from his faith to Christianity. In some countries, the Christian preacher may face a death penalty. Muslims believe they must claim the right to be building mosques everywhere in the West while it is legally unimaginable to allow churches in their own countries. It is a pretension of liberality and a serious mistake for our Lawmakers to take lightly the Islamic threats and terrorism in the West. If we take the attitude of 'live and let live' towards Islam, it will surely live; but it will live to destroy us!

The Right To Weep Aloud

Where Islam gets a foothold, it persecutes Christians and yet makes every attempt to silence the Church from commenting. It can wound and yet take away the right of the victim to cry. The Coptic Christians in Egypt have suffered continued persecution for centuries, and they are still under the same oppression of Muslims. In Nigeria alone in the last few years, many Christians have been slaughtered. Do we have the freedom to weep? Having succeeded in slitting the throat of my brother, will they also prevent me from crying aloud?

Who is afraid of dying? Who is afraid of a threat from any quarter? *"Who shall separate us from the love of Christ? Shall tribulation, or distress, or persecution, or famine, or nakedness, or peril, or sword? As it is written, For thy sake we are killed all the day long; we are accounted as sheep for the slaughter. Nay, in all these things we are more than conquerors through Him who loved us."* (Romans 8:35-37). Nigerian Christians cannot be afraid of death again. Muslims have already killed them in great numbers — so much so, that religious riots are no longer really newsworthy in Nigeria.

If Muslims had no basis in the Quran and the Hadith for their violence, we would regard them as extremists. That is one of the reasons why we have to study the god that is speaking in the Quran and that has inspired them against us. We thank our God that the blood of the Christian martyrs has always been the strength of the church of Christ. Shedding the blood of a child of God because of his faith, has often led to revival in the Church.

We are not afraid. We win by losing; we conquer by dying. Augustine, describing the experience of the early Christians, said: "The martyrs were bound, jailed, scourged, racked, burned, rent, butchered... and they multiplied." Hallelujah! This writer has worked in Nigeria and he can say that this, exactly, is what is happening in that land. More Muslims have been converted to Christianity in ten years of serious persecution than in all the past decades of dialogue put together. This is marvellous in our eyes. And now the devil is confused, regretting what he has done. But he has not seen anything yet. We are just starting.

This decade is very crucial in God's programme. Many attempts are being made to close doors to Christian ministry in many nations. But we are confident that now is the time that many of the captives of Islam in many seemingly impenetrable Islamic countries of the world will be set free by the power of the Holy Spirit. They may chain some of us but they cannot chain the Word of God. They may ban us from entering their country, but they cannot ban the Holy Spirit of God from penetrating and beginning to convict their captives.

All Islamic countries are in God's programme. They must all be represented in heaven (Revelation 7:9-10). But after the victory Jesus obtained for their salvation two thousand years ago, the devil is still holding them in the bondage of false religion and demonic influences. Billions have died in their sins and in a false hope. Any moment now, Christ will return to take his own, and God will release the cup of His wrath upon the world. But by His sovereignty, God is going to reach out to all these nations to save some by all means. He is going to do this because of His love. It is impossible for any security device to prevent this. It is impossible for persecution to prevent this. God is going to show Himself sovereign in these nations. Jesus said: "Go ye therefore, and teach (or make disciples of) all nations..." (Matthew 28:19). God is already giving us the necessary anointing and the required equipment to get the job done, and nothing can stop us. Speaking of rescuing the religiously enslaved folk, Jesus had said, "how can one enter into a strong man's house, and spoil his goods, except he first bind the strong man?" (Matthew 12:29), By the power of the Lord, and as God's Eagle Band, we are penetrating into the 'strongman's' bases to release his captives. "And it shall come to pass in that day, that his burden shall be taken away from off thy shoulder, and his *yoke from off thy neck, and the yoke shall be destroyed because of the anointing."* (Isaiah 10:27).

An Open Challenge

In our humble opinion, we don't think Muslims need to fight. Jesus had said, "I am the Way, the Truth, and the Life." The religious leaders of His days said, No. They crucified Him. But on the third day, He rose again, appeared to many in the very town of Jerusalem for forty full days before ascending to heaven bodily. He is still alive today in His majestic glory. This is to demonstrate that TRUTH has an inherent ability of defence and survival. As Christians, we have never been moved by the provocative Islamic pamphlets, audio and video cassettes of Ahmed Deedat and his elderly pupils in South Africa, and other parts of the world. We do not believe we have to make any noise or fight to defend the truth. Truth is always victorious.

Muslims, however, would want to defend Islam against criticism by any imaginable means. If the religion of Mohammed is 'the Truth' or even a truth of the Truth, Allah need not command that Muslims should take physical swords to preserve it. Jesus was crucified by fire-breathing Roman soldiers, yet He rose up again. I think the Islamic truth should be able to resurrect if crucified by mere writers. Let Muslims, therefore, relax and see what the printing press can do in crucifying their 'truth'.

Who is afraid of the pen and who is afraid of the press? The truth of the Christian faith has undergone pen crucifixion for many centuries now; yet it is still alive, spreading everywhere without the force of arms. There is no day that no one is converted to the Bible truth. It is only in countries with Christian orientation and influence that a man is free to think in the way he likes and to believe what he wants to believe. It is an offence to be a citizen of an Islamic country and believe and preach that Jesus is the Saviour. Christian literature and missionaries are not allowed. Why? If Muslims believe their 'truth' is invulnerable, let the Islamic world open its gates to Christian literature and to men and women, anointed and sent by the Holy Ghost, and let us see for the next decade what 'the Sword of the Spirit' can do to the heart of a Muslim in a free environment. Let us see what the anointing can do in breaking the yoke of falsehood. This is an open challenge! We don't need to fight.

Muslims write many things to attack the Christian faith. But they are made afraid when seeing a Christian approach the Quran with a critical knife. What we know is that a real truth is never afraid of a lie. It is a lie that fears the knowledge of the truth. That is why Christians are never afraid of a lie. We allow the mind to exercise itself to grasp the truth and then decide. No coercion. By the time one experiences the truth, one will never be afraid of a lie but simply deride it. It is a lie that will be afraid and suspicious of a revelation. This writer has read several books by agnostics, atheists, humanists, psychologists, communists and Muslim scholars. But an average Muslim is afraid of Christian literature. Someone tried to give the first edition of this book to a Muslim friend at the University of Reading, England. The Muslim student refused when he learnt that it was written by a Christian. Why? He was afraid he might be confronted with facts that may shatter his faith in Islam. The average Muslim is afraid even to touch Christian literature, especially, if it deals with Islam. He is even ready to slay the writer. Why? Because he wants to defend 'the truth'. But all we are saying is that truth, by its virtue, has the ability of defending itself! Moreover, a truth that is the truth is not the one that is worth killing for boldly, but the one that is worth dying for willingly. A religion that is not worth dying for is not worth living for; yet a religious man must be sure he is not dying in a lie or a deception. That is why a Muslim must be patient to examine what is being presented in this treatise about the Allah that is speaking in the Quran.

Let Allah Contend

We have to defend our faith and our beliefs against falsehood, but why should we defend God or try to save his reputation? The worst we can do to a person who blasphemes our God is hand him over to Him for an immediate judgment. That was what Paul did on the Island of Paphos when a false prophet and sorcerer, Elymas, was trying to prevent the chief of the island from being converted. He received instant blindness (Acts 13:6-12). God defended His Word there.

Late in 1987 a Muslim decided to bulldoze the graves of certain white Christian missionaries at Ibi town in the Wukari Local Government Area of the present Taraba State of Nigeria in order to extend his estate. God spoke to a Christian to tell the Emir of Ibi to warn the man. The Emir was reluctant because of his religious leanings. On December 24, the graves were bulldozed. Immediately, a mysterious fire broke out. The bulldozer was the first victim. After the bulldozer, the fire selectively burned the property of several Muslims in that town. Only little children could see the approach of the fire to any of its targets. The invisible fire continued until March the following year. By January, the fire had already gutted about 400 houses, according to a report by a Northern Nigerian based secular newspaper, *The Reporter*, of January 30, 1988. By March, the number of houses affected had grown to about 3,000.[15] Some Muslims

15 *Good News* magazine, April/May, 1988, Kaduna.

52

who had not been affected and were quick to realise that the fire was selective, went to hide their belongings in the nearby town and villages. But the fire could identify the properties from Ibi town and did justice to those properties leaving those of their hosts in the same houses intact! No Christians were affected. But a few Christians who dared sympathise with their Muslim friends immediately had a brush of the show. "A Muslim parent who beat his child for joining some Christians in a prayer meeting, had his house gutted that very evening."[16]

That sounds like a folktale in the 20th century? Yes, it is strange; but it was real. At least two secular newspapers reported this strange fire incident. At least three Christian publications reported it. Even the Nigerian Television Authority (NTA Lagos) reported it in the week-end programme *Newsline* and a committee of seismologists was set up by the Federal Government to investigate the cause and the extent of the damage of the mysterious fire. The Committee had no scientific explanation.

When all efforts, sacrifices and prayers sought by the Emir failed to stop the operation of the fire, and it became obvious that the Christian God was defending even the dry bones of His servants who had died as far back as 1904 and 1905. The Christians realised they must not sympathise with the Muslims, but they did not rejoice over what happened. All they did was to summon the people together and preach the gospel of peace and love to them. A Christian organisation, *Love Divine Ministry*, based in Kaduna was there. Over 400 people, most of them Muslims, were converted; and some of them came forward to say God had also healed them of certain physical diseases and disablement. The three-day visitation

16 Op. cit.

of the Holy Spirit in the area has been described as a rain of revival. We believe that people serving a great God do not have to defend such a God. A god worth the name should be able to defend himself and his followers. This reminds us of an event in the Old Testament which we can use to explain this further. When the people of Israel backslid and began to worship Baal, one of them, Gideon, rose up one night and destroyed the altar of Baal of which his father Joash was the priest. *"And when the men of the city arose early in the morning, behold, the altar of Baal was cast down, and the grove was cut down that was by it, and the second bullock was offered upon the altar that was built. And they said one to another, Who hath done this thing? And when they inquired and asked, they said, Gideon the son of Joash hath done this thing. Then the men of the city said unto Joash, Bring out thy son, that he may die: because he hath cast down the altar of Baal, and because he hath cut down the grove that was by it. And Joash said unto all that stood against him, Will ye plead for Baal? will ye save him? he that will plead for him, let him be put to death whilst it is yet morning: if he be a god, let him plead for himself, because one hath cast down his altar. Therefore on that day he called him Jerubbaal, saying, Let Baal plead against him, because he hath thrown down his altar."* (Judges 6:28-32).

We think the law of Joash, the priest of Baal, could be made an international law today: that whoever threatens the life of a blasphemer so-called should also be threatened; whoever kills, or promotes or instigates the killing of a supposed infidel or blasphemer or heretic should be killed. A nation that does so should be given a military sanction by a super-power. As far as we are concerned as Christians, we **do not have to defend our God.**

Muslims claim they can use violence if their god or prophet is blasphemed. If they are convinced a person is blaspheming their god or breaking down the altar of their religion through pen and paper, why don't they allow Allah to contend with the blasphemer? We think that would be the more religious thing to do. If Allah is a Saviour, why should they have to save him from the hand of an infidel? All they should do is to rename the kaferi 'Jerub-allah.' A God that needs to be fought for by weak human beings ceases to be the Almighty God. We therefore challenge our Muslim friends in all quarters to put down their cutlasses, swords, bombs and knives, matches and petrol, and let Allah fight his Christian enemies.

It Is A Sin To Help God!

There is the story of Uzzah in the Bible who wanted to help God. The ark of God was being carried on a cart to the City of David amidst 30,000 people singing and dancing: *"And when they came to Nachon's threshingfloor, Uzzah put forth his hand to the ark of God, and took hold of it; for the oxen shook it. And the anger of the LORD was kindled against Uzzah; and God smote him there for his error; and there he died by the ark of God"* (2 Samuel 6:6-7). You wonder what is happening? Here we see a zealous man who wanted to help the glory of God. He felt that God was about to be disgraced; he felt that God's reputation was at stake; he felt that the Lord who is enthroned between the cherubim in heaven could fall from His throne, and so *"Uzzah put forth his hand..."* and received instant judgment! Of course, God was not in the ark, but the ark represented His covenant with Israel and His glory. God can never fall from His throne! No idolater, no philosopher, no Islamic or non-Islamic writer can fell God.

If Muslims think their Allah is indeed God, let them allow him to defend himself and contend with his enemies. If Allah is God and Muslims are defending his reputation, they must know that they are incurring the wrath of God upon themselves. It is like saying, "Oh my, Allah is helpless and I must do something or his reputation will crumble." That would be irreverent!

CHAPTER THREE

The Wars In The Bible

READING through the Old Testament of the Bible, we find places where there are wars. One may ask: why were there wars if the God of the Bible, unlike Allah, is a God of peace?

The God of the Bible is indeed a God of love and peace; but He is also a God who has a special hatred for SIN because He is the holy God. His holiness demands swift judgment; yet He still bears long with man's wickedness.

He gave the Israelites strength to defeat the enemies that came against them, not necessarily because He has special interest in the Israelites (though He does and the Quran itself testifies to this in Surah 2:40, 47, 122), but mainly because He hated the sin and the wickedness of these other nations. The grace Israelites enjoyed in the Old Testament was because their forefathers — Abraham, Isaac, and Jacob, were friends of God. While many other people in different parts of the world gave themselves to idols, building images and calling them the God that made the heaven and the earth, the ancestors of the Israelites knew and followed the true God wholeheartedly. God says, *"Thou shalt not bow down thyself unto them, nor serve them: for I the LORD thy God am a jealous God, visiting the iniquity of the fathers upon the children unto the third and fourth generation of them that hate me, And shewing mercy unto thousands of them that love me and keep my commandments."* (Deuteronomy 5:9-10).

Some of the nations Israel fought against were destroyed because they were heathen who, instead of accepting the God of Israel, tempted Israel to worship idols (Numbers 25:1-9; 31:1-3). But even then, God did not instruct them to kill anybody they met on the way before reaching Canaan. There were so many unprintable sins these nations in Canaan were committing, and they easily influenced the Israelites to turn from the true God to idolatry, astrology, human sacrifices, and especially the sacrifice of their own children who were being burnt in the fire to the idol, Molech (Deuteronomy 12:30-31). Because of His holiness God also had to bring judgement on Israel for the sin these Moabite idolaters had lured them into. God had told Israel that if they started to indulge in such wickedness He Himself would punish them. In fact, Israel has suffered more for idolatry than any nation in the world. God has dealt with them more severely than their enemies because He chose to use them to reveal Himself to the world. But this privilege carried with it a great responsibility. There are many things that certain nations could do without any serious punishment from the Lord as a nation. But not so with Israel. Through the prophet Amos, God told Israel, *"Hear this word that the LORD hath spoken against you, O children of Israel, against the whole family which I brought up from the land of Eqypt, saying: "You only have I known of all the families of the earth; therefore I will punish you for all your iniquities."* (Amos 3:1-2). So, the issue of partiality did not come in.

Nearly all the wars the Israelites were involved in were inevitable. Most of these nations just hated them, as some nations do today. The first war the Israelites fought was because of a direct assault from the Amalekites. There was a shorter way from Egypt to Canaan, but the Amalekites were there and could fight them, and God didn't want Israel to fight at that time. So Moses took them through a hazardous wilderness to avoid any confrontation, but as they were resting at Rephidim, the Amalekites suddenly struck, determined to destroy Israel — unprovoked.

Moses sought the face of the Lord and then sent Joshua and some chosen men to the battle-field; and by the help of God, the Amalekites were defeated (Exodus 17:8-13). *"And the* LORD *said unto Moses, Write this for a memorial in a book, and rehearse it in the ears of Joshua: for I will utterly put out the remembrance of Amalek from under heaven."* (Exodus 17:14). It was for this that God later commanded King Saul to destroy the Amalekites. Many other nations which had heard of the fame of Israel's encounter in Egypt made up their mind to attack them whenever they heard of them coming through their land.

"Let us pass, I pray thee, through thy country: we will not pass through the fields, or through the vineyards, neither will we drink of the water of the wells: we will go by the king's high way, we will not turn to the right hand nor to the left, until we have passed thy borders." (Numbers 20:17). So Moses pleaded with the King of Edom, but he refused, and they had to turn back. *"And when king Arad the Canaanite, which dwelt in the south, heard tell* (news) *that Israel came by the way of the spies; then he fought against Israel, and took some of them prisoners. And Israel vowed a vow unto the* LORD, *and said, If thou wilt indeed deliver this people into my hand, then I will utterly destroy their cities. And the* LORD *harkened to the voice of Israel, and delivered up the Canaanites; and they utterly destroyed them and their cities"* (Numbers 21:1-3). That was the second war Israel fought after they left Egypt. Again, *"And Israel sent messengers unto Sihon, king of the Amorites, saying, Let me pass through thy land: we will not turn into the fields, or into the vineyards; we will not drink of the waters of the well: but we will go along by the king's high way, until we be past thy borders. And Sihon would not suffer Israel to pass through his border: but Sihon gathered all his people together, and went out against Israel into the wilderness: and he came to Jahaz, and fought against*

Israel. And Israel smote him with the edge of the sword, and possessed his land..." (Numbers 21:21-24). We should note that there are no wars in the New Testament between Christians and the heathen. The Christians subjected themselves to the cruelty of the rulers of their days. In fact, one of the reasons why the Jews rejected Jesus was because He did not prove to be the leader that would lead them in a war against their oppressors, the Romans.

It is very significant to note that in the Old Testament whenever Israel sinned and went to any battle, they lost and died. Joshua 7, the aftermath of Achen's sin, is a good example of this. After the death of Joshua, "*And the children of Israel did evil in the sight of the LORD, and served Baalim:. and provoked the LORD to anger. And they forsook the LORD and served Baal and Ashtaroth. And the anger of the LORD was hot against Israel, and he delivered them into the hands of spoilers that spoiled them, and he sold them into the hands of their enemies round about, so that they could not any longer stand before their enemies. Whithersoever they went out, the hand of the LORD was against them for evil, as the LORD had said, and as the LORD had sworn unto them: and they were greatly distressed.*" (Judges 2:11-15). It is therefore clear that even though God was with Israel, He is so holy He will NEVER tolerate sin in any circle — Israelite or non-Israelite. Whenever sin was in the camp of Israel, thousands of souls had to die for it. In the time of Moses, when they made a molten calf to represent the God that brought them out of Egypt, the Lord's anger burned against them and He made up his mind to finish them at a swoop, and wipe them off the surface of the earth forever! He would have done so but for the intercession of Moses: "*And I fell down before the LORD, as at the first, forty days and forty nights: I did neither eat bread, nor drink water, because of all your sins which ye sinned, in doing wickedly in the sight of the LORD, to provoke him to anger."* (Deuteronomy 9:18). Even though God did not destroy the whole of Israel that day, about 3,000 men died. (Exodus 32:28).

Any heathen nation or group of people — be it the most sophisticated or the most down-to-earth — who think they can ignore the creator and worship anything either from the culture of their forefathers, or of the creation (nature) itself should know that the fearful judgment of God is hanging upon them, no matter how long this may seem to take. *"Because sentence against an evil work is not executed speedily, therefore the heart of the sons of men is fully set in them to do evil"* (Ecclesiastes 8:11).

"These things hast thou done, and I kept silence; thou thoughtest that I was altogether such an one as thyself; but I will reprove thee, ... Now, consider this, you who forget God, lest I tear you in pieces and there be none to deliver." (Psalm 50:21-22). *"Though hand join in hand, the wicked* (sinner) *shall not be unpunished: but the seed of the righteous shall be delivered."* (Proverbs 11:21).

In case of any doubt, in Deuteronomy 9:1-5, God told the children of Israel that He was going to destroy the nations beyond the Jordan to the Promised Land. But Moses told them emphatically that it was on account of the wickedness of those nations: *"Not for thy righteousness, or for the uprightness of thine heart, dost thou go to possess their land: but for the wickedness of these nations the LORD your God doth drive them out from before thee, and that he may perform the word which the LORD sware unto thy fathers, Abraham, Isaac and Jacob."* (Deuteronomy 9:5).

Paul says: *"If God be for us, who can be against us?"* (Romans 8:31). However, Allah says fight against the Jews (Surah 9:29 Al Hilali). Allah sounds very much like the kings of the Amorites, the King of Jericho, Adonizedeck, and all those who rose against the Jews.

'Destroy the Jews' has been the cry of the heathen from Old Testament days, and is still heard today. That was the cry of Haman in Esther 3:8-9; it was the cry of Adolf Hitler when more than six million Jews were slaughtered because he did not want them to continue to exist. But thank God that the seed of Abraham shall never perish from the earth, no matter how fierce the animosity of the enemies of their God! The question still is: Who is this Allah that is so incensed against God's people? Who is this Allah that Hitler was echoing?

Jews were no idol worshippers. They held strictly to the Law God gave them through Moses. They even sometimes did more than the Law required, adding more burdens to themselves! Whenever they were ensnared to worship an idol, God had a way of punishing them to bring them back to their senses. Jews have been the people who have suffered most in the world as a nation — from their 430 years of slavery in Egypt up to today. Yet it has pleased the Lord that the Saviour of the world should come through them. That is the decision of the Lord and there is nothing anybody can do about it, *"for salvation is of the Jews"* (John 4:22).

CHAPTER FOUR
The Christian Warfare

CHRISTIANITY is warfare. But its warfare begins and ends at the Cross of Christ, and the victory announced at His resurrection.

The famous Arabic poet, Ahmad Shawgi, embarrassed the Muslim world when he wrote in one of his collections how Jesus fought and won through different means from that of the Muslims. He says the Cross was wood, not iron with a sharp edge. And speaking again in another poem written as a tribute to Christ on a Christmas day, he says: "Essa, your way, mercy and love, of innocence among men, and peace as a dove. You were not the one to shed blood, nor one that neglected the weak, nor the orphan." (Translated by F. Barsoum).

One thing about us is that we are servants of the God of the Bible. We do not have many enemies: we have only one enemy, Satan, and he has already been defeated by the Cross and the Resurrection. All others — humans and demons — are just his servants and agents, and we know how best to deal with them. According to the gospel of Jesus Christ, the Son of God, *"the servant of the Lord must not strive; but be gentle to all men, apt to teach, patient, In meekness instructing those that oppose themselves; if God peradventure will give them repentance to the acknowledging of the truth; And that they may recover themselves out of the snare of the devil, who are taken captive by him at his will."* (2 Timothy 2:24-26).

It is not even because we have such teachings that we do not fight physically. It is rather because we have *"the mind of Christ"* (1 Corinthians 2:16). The Quran itself has acknowledged Christians as loving everybody, and even their Muslim enemies! (Surah 5:82-85).

That is our calling. It is no weakness. *"That ye may be the children of your Father which is in heaven: for he maketh his sun to rise on the evil and on the good, and sendeth rain on the just and on the unjust."* (Matthew 5:45). Our God is a God of love, and according to the Scriptures, *"the love of God is shed abroad in our hearts by the Holy Ghost"* (Romans 5:5) at the time of our conversion. This kind of love cannot be faked, neither can anyone have it except he is born of, and by, the Spirit. Even if Muslims fake many things in Christianity, they can't fake our love. Hallelujah!

Jesus told some religious people: *"I speak that which I have seen with my Father: and ye do that which ye have seen with your father. They answered and said unto him, Abraham is our father. Jesus saith unto them, If ye were Abraham's children, ye would do the works of Abraham. But now ye seek to kill me, a man that hath told you the truth, which I have heard of God: this did not Abraham. Ye do the deeds of your father. Then said they to him, We be not born of fornication; we have one Father, even God. Jesus said unto them, If God were your Father, ye would love me: for I proceeded forth and came from God; neither came I of myself, but he sent me...Ye are of your father the devil, and the lusts of your father ye will do. He was a murderer from the beginning, and abode not in the truth, because there is no truth in him. When he speaketh a lie, he speaketh of his own; for he is a liar, and the father of it"* (John 8:38-42,44).

The Bible, no doubt talks of Christians fighting and warring. But it makes sufficiently clear that *"We wrestle not against flesh and blood, (physical human beings) but against principalities, against powers, against the rulers of the darkness of this world, against spiritual wickedness in high places."* and therefore, *"the weapons of our warfare are not carnal, (physical arm, cutlasses, swords, guns, knives, matches and petrol, bows and arrows)* *but **mighty** through God to the pulling down of strong-holds;"* (Ephesians 6:12 & 2 Corinthians 10:4).

During the religious crises in Northern Nigeria, a section of the press gave the impression that both Muslims and Christians were fighting. The assumption was that it must take two to fight. Nothing could be farther from the truth. If Christians had reacted accordingly, there would have been another terrible civil war in Nigeria. Christians do protest verbally sometimes, but we have a teaching from our Lord to turn the other cheek, and this guides us in the face of all provocations. It is the Lord's doing to turn our enemies against themselves, and then save some of them into His fold. And we thank God for what He is doing in Northern Nigeria now in terms of conversions from Islam.

We have never been moved by the provocative Islamic pamphlets, videos and cassettes of Ahmed Deedat and his elderly pupils in many places. We do not believe we have to defend the truth. Truth is always victorious.

Yes, we win without any noise and without physical weapons. The Apostle Paul enumerated all the six weapons of the Christian warfare, namely: the **belt** of truth buckled around (our) waist with the **breastplate** of righteousness (holiness) in place; our feet fitted with the readiness (**soldiers' boots**) that comes from (preaching) the gospel of peace. In addition to all this, taking up the **shield** of faith with which we extinguish all the flaming arrows (dangerous teachings) of the evil one (that can destroy our faith). Taking up the **helmet** of salvation and the **sword** of the spirit, which is the Word of God, and always praying in the spirit. (Ephesians 6:10-18). The imagery evoked here is that of a Roman soldier, but it is clear from the passage that none of these weapons is physical. They are all spiritual.

Jesus Christ rebuked Peter who used a physical sword to defend Him, and then restored the ear that was severed, making Peter realise that His not fighting physically did not mean He was weak. But that the weapons of the Christian warfare are **MIGHTY THROUGH GOD**, and therefore, more powerful than any physical thing. Moreover, He surrendered himself to be killed not because His enemies were stronger, but so that His followers would know: *"Therefore doth my Father love me, because I lay down my life, that I might take it again. No man taketh it from me, but I lay it down of myself. I have power to lay it down, and I have power to take it again. This commandment have I received of my Father"* (John 10:17-18). He said this a long time before He died.

What About The Crusades?

We are not ignorant of the history of the Crusades that took place from 1096 till the early 13th Century to regain Jerusalem from Arab and Turkish Muslims. These wars were generally regarded as wars between Christians and Muslims. But the fact that they were wars between Europe and the Islamic and Turkish rulers did not make them religious. The assumption was that 'Christian' Europe was warring against the Muslims. The Crusades in history were political wars engineered by kings and emperors and the apostate papacy who wanted to annexe Jerusalem, but felt the Turks had beaten them to it. Apart from the terrible loss of lives — including children — Peter the Hermit, Godfrey of Bouillion, Gottschalk and all their Crusaders, including the Catholic Pope Urban II who engineered the whole thing, failed because the wars were not God's wars. The Christian God can't lose a battle. Even though the Crusaders went out with the sign of the cross, yet these fighters were not Christians; they neither knew nor obeyed the Scriptures.

Jesus had said: *"...and Jerusalem shall be trodden down of the Gentiles, until the times of the Gentiles be fulfilled"* (Luke 21:24). Here, Jesus was explaining to His true disciples what was going to happen to the Holy Land because it had rejected His Lordship. He said it was a punishment *"that all things which are written may be fulfilled"* (Luke 21:22), and therefore warned the disciples to make sure they flee when things begin to happen.

Daniel and the Lord Jesus prophesied *"...the abomination of desolation."* (The reader is advised to go back to the Bible and read Luke 21:20-24 and Daniel 11:31 for a better understanding of the matter). The fulfilment of these prophecies started in A.D. 70 when General Titus, following his father Vespasian, invaded the Holy Land and destroyed the most cherished Temple, and Jews were dispersed all over the world.

Barely six years after the death of Mohammed, in 638 A.D., Mohammed's followers also came with swords and conquered Jerusalem and occupied it. It is recorded that when Jerusalem finally fell, over 90,000 "Christians" were slaughtered by these invaders.

Today, you find the Mosque of Omar at a site very near that of the former majestic and glorious Solomon's Temple, where, instead of the cloud of the glory of Jehovah, we hear regular chants of la illaha to Allah. That Mosque took half a century to complete.

Jews who yearn for God, still go to a place near the Temple site to wail for their sins beside the Wailing Wall. Muslims, not satisfied with encroaching on the Temple Mount, frequently hail stones from inside the Mosque at the praying Israelis around the Wailing Wall. This had been going on for a long time and nobody seemed to notice. On October 8, 1990, the provocation reached a new stage and the Israeli police had to

67

open fire on the Muslims, killing 21. This sparked off condemnation from the International Community.

Another imposing mosque, El-Aksa Mosque, was erected on Abraham's grave at Hebron. The Christians' most holy place on earth, the top of Mount Calvary, where the Son of God shed His holy blood, has become a Muslim cemetery! Near this is Golgotha which became a busy Arab bus station!

As students of Bible prophecy, we believe that this constitutes *"the abomination of desolation, spoken of by Daniel the prophet, standing where it ought not"* as Jesus prophesied in Mark 13:14. But one thing is clear in the Bible, and that is: *"the time of the Gentiles"* will surely expire in all these places — and that very soon. We know part of this has been fulfilled and is still being fulfilled before our very eyes. As for the final dissolution of these Gentiles in this ancient holy city, it is the Spirit of the Lord Himself that will raise a standard against His enemies.

As for Christians, our weapons of warfare are greater than any atomic bomb the world can ever dream of inventing. The "Crusades" of today mean rescuing souls from the hand of the devil and turning them over to the Lord, for *"Knowing therefore the terror of the Lord, we persuade men"* (2 Corinthians 5:11) to turn away from sin and false religions and receive the gift of Salvation offered in Christ Jesus .

It is significant to recall here that King David, in his pietistic zeal, nursed the idea of building that great temple for the Lord, but then explained: *"But God said unto me, Thou shalt not build an house for my name, because thou hast been a man of war, and hast shed blood"* (1 Chronicles 28:3).

That is the God of the Bible! And we can be sure He is completely different from the god of the combative prophet Mohammed.

Many early mosques built by Mohammed and his successors and even the mosque of Omar standing almost at the site of that Temple were built with hands of blood; and Allah delights in that and promises them rewards in heaven. Yet people say we are worshipping the same God and going to the same heaven!

Muslim scholars may assume smartness to advance a lot of arguments to defend their religion, but they can't escape the facts of their history. Facts are invincible; no intellectual arguments can demolish them.

The Muslims' Weapons Against Satan

Any religion that is of the true God will have Satan as an adversary who must be fought against with the strongest weapons available. Muslims also see Satan as an enemy that should be fought.

But how do they fight him? With what weapons? The recommendation of Mohammed is stones and pebbles! (Bukhari Vol. 9 No. 336). That is why every Muslim pilgrim who performs the Hajj to Mecca must pick seven pebbles to throw at the pillar called The Great Satan. What are we to think of such a direction from Allah's prophet? Throwing pebbles at a spirit! Incredible! Surely Allah knew better than that!

As for Christians, the Word of God, the Bible, has made it clear that our warfare is not against a being of flesh and blood that can be stoned. Therefore it does not recommend physical weapons to fight the devil and his hosts: *"For the weapons of our warfare are not carnal, but mighty through God to the pulling down of strongholds* (of the devil); *Casting down imaginations, and every high thing that exalteth itself against the knowledge of God, and bringing into captivity every thought to the obedience of Christ"* (2 Corinthians 10:4-5).

One is surprised to note here that while Allah recommends pebbles to fight the devil[1] he commands that Christians and Jews be fought against and converts be slain (Surah 4:89). Is this suggesting that believers in Christ Jesus are more dangerous than the devil himself? This is significant, and it is one of many reasons why we have to know the answer to the question: Who is this Allah?

---

1 See Ali, Yusuf, *Quran, Text, Translation and Commentary* Note 217 (6)

CHAPTER FIVE
Allah And The Sonship Of Jesus

"Who hath ascended up into heaven, or descended? who hath gathered the wind in his fists? who hath bound the waters in a garment? who hath established all the ends of the earth? what is his name, and what is his son's name, if thou canst tell?" (Proverbs 30:4).

"For we have not followed cunningly devised fables, when we made known unto you the power and coming of our Lord Jesus Christ, but were eyewitnesses of his majesty. For he received from God the Father honour and glory, when there came such a voice to him from the excellent glory, This is My beloved Son, in whom I am well pleased. And this voice which came from heaven we heard, when we were with him in the holy mount. We have also a more sure word of prophecy; whereunto ye do well that ye take heed, as unto a light that shineth in a dark place, until the day dawn and the day star arise in your hearts:" (2 Peter 1:16-19).

THE relationship of Jesus Christ with God has been the major offence to Muslims and the problem of Allah himself. Is Jesus the Son of God? Can God have a Son? The Bible says, yes. Allah says, no.

Because Christians insist that Jesus is the Son of the living God, the Quran says, "God's curse be on them...!"(Surah 9:30).

It is impossible for a Muslim to believe all the words of the Quran and still believe that Jesus is the Son of God. Someone may ask: Was it Mohammed that personally developed a hatred for this fundamental truth of the Christian faith or the Allah that was inspiring him?

Some have suggested that, initially, Mohammed had good intentions and that he only fell helplessly

71

into the hand of a malicious *jinn* who deceived him and stood him up against the Sonship and deity of Jesus Christ.

For example, the Allah of pre-Islamic Mecca was said to have had sons and daughters. Mohammed might have felt this was improper for a Creator. Maybe that was why we hear: "The primal origin of the heavens and the earth: How can He have a son when He hath no consort?" (Surah 6:101).

This Meccan paganistic teaching was probably the idea Mohammed was against. But when he heard that the Almighty God of the Christians also has a Son called Jesus, he dismissed the idea together with the Meccans' idea of the 'fatherhood' of God as heresy.

Another confusion that cropped up at the time of Mohammed was the doctrine of the Mary-amiyya cults prevalent between the 5th century A.D. and the end of the 7th century A.D. These sectaries were pagans who had believed the creator had a Wife called Venus or Al Zahrah whom they regarded as 'the Queen of Heaven', and that they had a son by procreation. When these people were converted (or rather diverted) to Christianity, they imported the doctrine into the church, regarding Mary as the Venus or Al-Zahrah, the 'Queen of Heaven', and Jesus as the son. They exalted and worshipped Mary as a goddess, hence they were called the Marianists.

Genuine Christians felt this was a dangerous doctrine, and fought the heresy and excommunicated the adherents. Before the end of the 7th century A.D., the sects existed no more.

This was the period when Islam emerged. Maybe that is why we read that the Christian Trinity consists of God the Father, Mary and Jesus. (Surah 5:119). It is either that Mohammed took the

Marianist doctrine as the Christian doctrine of Trinity or that he was altogether ignorant of what Christians believed about the Holy Trinity and particularly, the Sonship of Jesus. It has also been said that the veneration of Mary by the Roman Catholics might have compounded the confusion of Mohammed in this regard. Nestorian and Arian heresies were also ripe among Christians at the time of Mohammed, thus contributing to his confusion.

But we must be very careful not to draw a conclusion yet. The issue is more complex than that. The evidence that Mohammed's repudiation of the Sonship of Jesus·was because of the Meccan and Maria-mist doctrines is very slender. It is only from some historical records we can suggest such a conclusion; and it is only a suggestion. From the Quran itself, how-ever, it is evident that apart from the idolaters of Mecca, Mohammed deliberately opposed Bible Christianity in particular as a form of heathenism. Worshipping Jesus as the Son of God was seen as idolatry. It is the same thing happening today. The very idea of the Incarnation was unimaginable to Mohammed, and still is to Muslims today.

The second problem is the issue of inspiration. If Mohammed insisted that it was Allah speaking through him, then we must take the matter very seriously. If he said he was being inspired by Allah to go against the Christian belief in the deity of Jesus, it would be from that perspective that we could approach the issue. If Allah is indeed "All-wise, All-knowing" as is repeated everywhere in the Quran, one would expect that he should know the real things that Christianity teaches. For example, the Christian doctrine of the Trinity does not include Mary. It is the Father, the Son and the Holy Spirit, and not the Father, Mary, and Jesus as is alleged in the Quran. (Surah 5:119).

From the Quran, the problem of the Allah of Mohammed was not as much the Trinity as the Sonship of Jesus. He hates it. In Surah 19:88-89, we read: "They say: '(God) Most Gracious has begotten a Son!' Indeed ye have put forth a thing most monstrous!". "Say: He is God The One and Only; God, the Eternal, Absolute; He begetteth not, nor is He begotten; And there is none like unto Him." (Surah 112). This is usually the key Surah for all Muslims.

"It befits not (the Majesty of) Allah that He should beget a son (this refers to the slander of Christians against Allah by saying that Jesus is the son of Allah). Glorified (and Exalted be He above all that they associate with Him). When He decrees a thing, He only says to it, 'Be!' — and it is." (Surah 19:35, Al Hilali et al).

There are several other places in the Quran where the sonship of Jesus is outrightly denied in strong and plain terms. Bringing Jesus onto the pedestal of Sonship to God is the unforgivable sin Muslims call 'shirk'. It irks them; it bites them; it annoys them; it nauseates them. They can't imagine it; it is simply impossible.

It is because certain things of God cannot be imagined that they are called 'wonderful'. God ceases to be God if His nature and all things He is capable of doing were only the things that can be logically reasoned out by the human mind.

Allah is quoted in the Quran as saying: "...the Christians call Christ the Son of God...God's curse be on them: how they are deluded away from the Truth!" (Surah 9:30).

Of course, there is no Allah's curse or charms that can affect a real born again Bible believing Christian, and maybe that is why Muslims take to physical weapons against us. We do not want to regret that Jesus is not the Son of Allah. It is indeed hard to imagine the Muslim god begetting "the Prince of Peace", or a "meek and lowly" Christ.

But let us see if there is any logic in the claim of the deity of Jesus. The Bible says, 'God is Spirit'. The Quran says Jesus is the Spirit of God that came into Mary, His mother. (Surah 21:91).

If God is Spirit and Jesus is the Spirit of God (and we agree that the spirit and the body are distinct yet one), then we do not need a *modus tollendo ponem* or any complex logic to conclude that Jesus is one with God. We should also remember that another name of Jesus given to Him 700 years before He was born physically, is Immanuel, meaning, 'God with us'.

Jesus did not become what He is because He was born of Mary. He had been what He is before the foundation of the world. He only incarnated, that is, took on the flesh of man because He wanted to save man. He emanated from God. When He came down, He said: *"Sacrifice and offering thou wouldest not, but a body hast thou prepared me:"* (Hebrews 10:5). He came down only to enter that body of Mary.

Again, the Bible says Jesus is the Word of God: *"In the beginning was the Word, and the Word was with God, and the Word was God ...And the Word was made flesh, and dwelt among us, (and we beheld his glory, the glory as of the only begotten of the Father,) full of grace and truth"* (John 1:1, 14).

In Surah 3:45, we read: "the angels said: 'O Mary! God giveth thee Glad tidings of a Word from Him: His name will be Christ Jesus, the son of Mary'". But because many Muslim commentators don't want to believe in anything that may suggest the deity of Jesus, they have suggested that 'the Word' is just the creative command (wish) of God, 'be'. But Muslim scholars in the class of Al Shaikh

Muhyl Al Din Al Arabi know better.[1] Al Arabi points out that the Arabic word translated 'whose' in that ayah is 'ismihi'. It is a masculine personal pronoun. That is why the English translation has rightly used the personal relative pronoun 'whose'. This shows that the Word being spoken about is not just a grammatical unit, or even a power, but a person. Celebrated Muslim scholar Al'Arasi wrote: "The Word is God in theophany ... and it is the one divine person."

Now, if the Word is a person, and the Word is God, and the Word became flesh, it means God became flesh. This means that it is not the case that Jesus, a mere man, made himself to be God, or Christians make him so, but that God made Himself to be in Jesus, and calls him His Son, His Christ.

In Surah 6:101, quoted earlier, we read: "The primal origin of the heavens and the earth: How can He have a son when He hath no consort?" Our attention should be drawn here to the fact that this is a person other than "the Lord" speaking... contrary to the claim of Muslims that all the words in the Quran are words being spoken by 'the Lord'.

But in Hadith Kudsi, the Lord is quoted as saying, "The rich are my agents and the poor are members of my family (my sons)."[2] This also disproves the Muslims' claim that the Hadith contains only the words and deeds of Mohammed as opposed to the Quran which contains the words of Allah.

Now, the writer of the Quran says, "When he did not have a wife?" But in that Hadith, Allah himself talks of "my family". As Christians, we do not take Allah having a family to mean that he is a husband with a wife, children, in-laws, etc. We understand that statement in the Hadith to be only

1 Arabi's book, *'Fusua al Hukum'* pp.13,35

2 Cited in Zachariah, Brutus, God is One — In the Holy Trinity, Rikon, Switzerland p.25.

metaphoric. But if Muslims have such a statement in one of their sacred books, why do they have to object so strongly to the idea of the Christian God having a Son? Why do they have to imagine the sonship of Jesus as a biological relationship?

We wish to say therefore that God is the Father of Jesus Christ, not in a physical sense, not even in the sense of the Hadith quoted above, but in a very special and unique way that transcends human comprehension. And it is because He is the Son of God that He is God in nature. God declares Jesus is His Son, and we will rather believe it than rationalise it. It is pride and arrogance for man to insist he must understand everything before accepting its reality. It is when we receive the Christian truth by simple faith that we begin to have a revelation of that truth in our spirit. Like the philosopher Anselm, what I can simply say is: credo ut intelligam ('I believe so that I may understand.') Jesus said, *"If any man will do his will, he shall know of the doctrine..."* (John 7:17).

This is to say that the Deity of Jesus as the Son of God is not necessarily a simple logically provable doctrine, and it doesn't have to be. We believe it because God says so, and that settles it. Yet on the other hand, this does not mean there is no sense in the doctrine, just as we have pointed out. With mordant invective, many Muslims tell us, "Look, you don't reason; an ordinary nursery school pupil knows elementary arithmetic and $1+1+1 = 3$ and not 1". We agree that $1+1+1 = 3$; but that is only in elementary arithmetic of nursery pupils. In advanced mathematics, physics and logic, $1+1+1$ CAN be 1 ! If many Muslims are really open to reason, they won't take the doctrine of the Trinity as offensive to logic. General Ibrahim Babangida of Nigeria, himself born a Muslim, has written: "The confirmation and concession by the Muslims that Jesus Christ was indeed of virgin birth leaves the door open for many possibilities. Two of these possibilities are in fact the divinity of Jesus Christ and his divine sonship." Philosophy agrees that there can be many in one and one manifesting many particulars just as mathematics allows that a set can have classes and subsets. The human body is a perfect example of many in one and one in many both in the philosophical and mathematical senses.

While the statement above of General Ibrahim Babandiga is a welcome appeal to reason and tolerance, the Bible teaches us that the question of the Person and Work of Jesus Christ must be settled in the heart and life of each individual while he is on earth. It will be too late for us to discover the truth on the Day of Judgement to our eternal loss and regret. But God has given us the intellect here on earth with which to reason. It is when people ignore reason they are open to emotionalism should their faith be critically examined. Yet God does not want us to have just an intellectual agreement with His Word. Our knowledge in the mind must lead us to a saving faith in the heart which must lead us to a changed life NOW. Veteran American Christian author Homer Duncan has said thousands of people miss Heaven by a few inches! "By this I mean the distance between the head and the heart."

God has indeed created man in His own image, according to the Bible. As a Trinity, He made man also a kind of trinity — spirit, soul and body, distinct yet one. This is wonderful. If the nature of man is a mystery, how much more the nature of God?

"And without controversy great is the mystery of godliness: (i.e. the divine nature or the Arabic 'uqnum') *God was manifest in the flesh, justified in the Spirit, seen of angels, preached unto the Gentiles, believed on in the world, received up into glory."* (1 Timothy 3:16).

That is the summary of the New Testament Bible. It was God that sent the angel Gabriel to announce to Mary: *"The Holy Ghost shall come upon thee, and the power of the Highest shall overshadow thee: therefore also that Holy One which shall be born of thee shall be called the Son of God."* (Luke 1:35).

Six hundred and forty years later, Mohammed said an angel Gabriel came to him with a message from an Allah that Jesus was not really what the Bible says He is, and that He was just a fine prophet. The question is: Which Gabriel, and whose Gabriel came to him? (He also said the Holy Spirit is the Angel Gabriel. Call that a confusion if you like.)

Before Mohammed came with his message, however, the Apostle Paul had already warned: *"But though we, or an angel from heaven, preach any other gospel unto you than that which we have preached unto you, let him be accursed."* (Galatians 1:8).

The reason is that it is only an angel of the devil that can say a thing contrary to what God had already said with His own voice from heaven in the presence of many witnesses when He declared, *"Thou art my beloved Son; in thee I am well pleased."* (Luke 3:22). Yes, God declared Jesus to be His Son. But Allah and his Mohammed say He cannot be, and that the aspects of the Scriptures that present Jesus as the Son of God are the adulterated Scriptures. The Bible says, *"let God be true, but every man a liar;"* (Romans 3:4).

A Muslim who truly believes in the Quran cannot believe that God can be so helpless in His world that He allows His Word to be corrupted. According to Surah 6:34, and 10:64, corruption of the Word of God is utterly impossible. God is in control of His Word. Everything the Bible says about Jesus is true. Nothing is untrue, and no fact is changed.

Muslim critics, commenting on the many different Bible Translations today, pretend they don't know that there are about 50 different translations of their own Quran too. In writing this book, I have read at least six translations of the Quran honoured by the majority of Muslims.

The only reason why Muslims claim that the Bible is corrupted is because it speaks of the deity of Christ. They say they cannot bow down for 'the Man of Galilee'. Their reason: that Jesus was a created being just as Adam was, and is no more a son of God than Adam was (Surah 3:59). Let us accept this for the sake of the following argument.

The Quran says in not less than eight places that when Adam was created, God commanded all angels to bow down and worship the man He had made: "We said to the angels, 'Bow down to Adam'; and they bowed down: not so Iblis: he refused and was haughty: He was of those who reject Faith". (Surah 2:34; Surah 7:11ff; Surah 15:29-35; Surah 17:61-62; Surah 18:50; Surah 20:115ff and Surah 38:71ff). In other words, what made Iblis an unbeliever was his refusal to bow for Adam. In Surahs 15 and 38, God released some curses on Iblis for this arrogance. The question is: If Muslims were on earth at that time would they too have bowed down for Adam? And would that not be un-Islamic? That is an axe for them to grind.

In 1 Corinthians 15:45, 47, the Bible says Jesus is the last Adam (though not in the Islamic sense.) *"And so it is written, The first man Adam was made a living soul; the last Adam was made a quickening spirit...The first man is of the earth, earthy: the second Man is the Lord from heaven."* No honest Muslim can deny any of these claims of the Bible. Adam was dust. But according to the Quran itself, Jesus Christ is not dust but the Word of God (khalimatullah) and a Spirit from God. God is quoted in the Quran as speaking of Jesus as

"Our Spirit" (Surah 21:91). We ask: Is God's own Spirit a separate entity or part of Him? And is this Spirit divine or not? That is an axe for them to grind.

Now, if the first Adam, mere dust, must be worshipped, even by angels, why not the last Adam, God's life-giving Spirit? With all humility, therefore, we say that if Muslims refuse to bow for the last Adam, it means they have joined forces with rebellion and arrogance with Iblis, and they are under the same curse released on Satan.

There are even some sincere Muslims who say they actually believe in Jesus. But that is not really true. What do they believe about Him? You see, one may believe in an historical 'Jesus', a man of Galilee, one of the prophets of God, a great teacher who spoke in parables, a good man who treated his neighbours right, produced bread and other miracles. Yes, it is possible for one to believe all this and yet miss it, if it ends there. If you are a Muslim, the devil would want you to believe every other thing in the Bible except the Sonship and Lordship of Jesus.

The Lord once asked His disciples, *"Whom do men say that I The Son of man am?"* The answer to that question is very important because our salvation lies there. A Muslim would say, 'He is one of the mightiest messengers of God; no more;' but there he misses it! Jesus is more than a prophet. Peter's answer was: *"Thou art the Christ, the Son of the living God"* (Matthew 16:16), and Jesus said it took a revelation of God for Peter to know this in his heart and confess it. If a Muslim has a problem in this regard, he can pray here and ask God to open his mind and heart to understand this.

John said he wrote his gospel, *"that ye might believe that Jesus is the Christ, the Son of God; and that believing ye might have **life through his name**."* (John 20:31).

Believing Jesus means believing in His Name; and His Name means 'Jehovah our salvation' or 'our Saviour'. So, a Muslim who does not believe that Jesus is man's salvation, cannot say he believes in Jesus. Salvation is in the belief in His name; and it is the Name that speaks of His Lordship.

Scripture says, *"Believe on the Lord Jesus Christ, and thou shalt be saved."* (Acts 16:31). That means you don't just believe in 'Jesus', but 'The Lord Jesus Christ'. That is, your Lord, and God's Christ. That is the simple faith that can do the supernatural work of changing your heart and making you right with God. Your believing only means agreeing with God. Refusal simply means pride.

Now, if you are a Muslim, do you want to agree with God or do you want to depend on your small reasoning and remain in your sins? Do you know what Jesus says in that regard? He says, *"..for if ye believe not that I am he, ye shall die in your sins."* (John 8:24). *"For there are three that bear record in heaven, the Father, the Word, and the Holy Ghost, and these three are one.. If we receive the witness of men, the witness of God is greater: for this is the witness of God which he hath testified of His Son. He that believeth on the Son of God hath the witness in himself: he that believeth not God hath made him a liar; because he believeth not the record that God gave of His Son. And this is the record, that God hath given to us eternal life, and this life is in His Son. He that hath the Son hath life, and he that hath not the Son of God hath not life."* (1 John 5:7, 9-12).

CHAPTER SIX

The Muslim Heaven

MANY people wonder why it is that Christians and Muslims claim to be heading to get to a particular heaven and yet are totally at odds about the way to get to that heaven.

A thorough study of the Quran shows, however, that the Christian heaven is different from the Muslim Paradise, despite the general euphoria and felicity both of them promise. In this chapter, we shall try to examine the Muslim heaven in comparison with the heaven of the Bible, and see how this can help us in identifying Allah, the God of the Muslim heaven.

Entrance To Heaven

The Quran says, "Those who avoid great sins and shameful deeds, only (falling into) small faults, verily thy Lord is ample in forgiveness." (Surah 53:32). That is to say, a sinner will enter the Muslim heaven if his sins are not too big!

This is clearly different from the heaven where God is. It is also different from where Christ will dwell when He comes back to reign. The only way to God is a way of complete holiness, "..*without which no man shall see the Lord*" (Hebrews 12:14). The Bible says: "*And an highway shall be there, and a way, and it shall be called The way of holiness; the unclean shall not pass over it*" (Isaiah 35:8, Revelation 21:27).

God is a holy God, and He is the God of the Christian heaven. He is a God who is "*of purer eyes than to behold* (approve of) *evil, and canst not look on iniquity:* (no matter how small it is)" (Habakkuk 1:13). However, He has made a provision for everyone who wills and is ready to humble himself to receive that provision.

Life In The Muslim Heaven.

The Quran, said to be a revelation of Allah, implies there will be a lot of marriages and sex in heaven (Surah 56:10-38 Al Hilali). The book talks of maidens "...whom no man or jinn *yatmithhunna* (has opened their hymens with sexual intercourse) before them." (Surah 55:56 Al Hilali). They are "pure wives" (Surah 3:15 Al Hilali) and 'wide-eyed houris' (Surah 37:48; Surah 44:50-55 A.J. Aberry). One Hadith says: "The lowliest of the inhabitants of paradise will be he who has eighty thousand servants, seventy-two wives..." (Mishkat al Masabih, Sh. M. Ashraf (1990) p.1204). Lest anyone should spiritualise this, Anas reported the Prophet as saying: "In paradise the believer will be given such power to conduct sexual intercourse" (Ibid. p.1200). No wonder Allah says his followers can multiply wives here on earth. We don't know whether he intends that polygamy here is to serve as a training ground for the Great Beyond.

We may profit from a brief flashback into the life of Mohammed, the prophet himself. Varying figures have been given in the Traditions as to the number of Mohammed's wives. Some say 27; some 29; some say 9; some 11 and some, 13. The problem is that there were so many of them, and new ones were acquired after nearly every war fought by his army. Later these women were kept in purdah. It is difficult for a biographer to give a precise and indisputable figure for the wives of the prophet of Islam. The wives we can specifically mention are: Aisha (Ayesha), Hafsa, Safia, Sawda, Um Salama, Zainab, Mariam, Ummu Habiba, Maymuna, Raihana, Juwayriyya and Safiyya. Ali Dashti gave more names.

The Quran itself gives us an idea about the scope of the privileges of women that Mohammed enjoyed in his time. In Surah 33:50, we read: "O Prophet! We have made lawful to thee thy wives to whom thou hast paid their dowers; and those whom thy right hand possesses out of the prisoners of war whom God has assigned to thee; and daughters of thy paternal uncles and aunts, and daughters of thy maternal uncles and aunts, who migrated (from Mecca) with thee, and any believing woman who dedicates her soul to the Prophet if the Prophet wishes to wed her; this only for thee, and not for the Believers (at large);".

However in spite of all the women that seem to have surrounded Mohammed he had no surviving male child. He therefore adopted a boy, Zaid ibn Harithah, as his son. Zaid grew up and was blessed with a charming young lady, Zainab whose name we have already mentioned. Unfortunately, this lady turned out to be a temptation to the prophet.

One day, on a visit to Zaid's house, Mohammed saw Zainab not completely covered. Overwhelmed and slain by the woman's beauty, the prophet gasped: **"Praise** belongeth unto Allah, who turneth the hearts of men as he willeth." Before long, arrangements were completed for Zaid to divorce Zainab so that the prophet could marry her.

At first, Mohammed feared what people would say if he seduced Zainab. So, he pretended he was not personally interested in the lady. But Allah rebuked him for such seeming hypocrisy and fear: "..thou didst say to one (Zaid)...'retain thou (in wedlock) thy wife, and fear God.' But thou (Mohammed) didst hide in thy heart that which God was about to make manifest: thou didst fear the people, but it is more fitting that thou shouldst fear God". (Surah 33:37).

What is being said in essence is this: If I am the one that turned your heart toward the beauty of Zaid's wife, why are you afraid of men in taking the right decision? Do you fear men more than you fear me?

Mohammed therefore yielded to the will of Allah and took Zainab to be his own wife.

No, the drama wasn't regarded as a sin. Two revelations came from Allah to justify the action for posterity. One of them is the one partly quoted in Surah 33:37. It continues: "Then when Zaid had dissolved (his marriage) with her, with the necessary (formality), We (Allah) joined her in marriage to thee: in order that (in future) there may be no difficulty to the Believers in (the matter of) marriage with the wives of their adopted sons, when the latter have dissolved with the necessary (formality) (their marriage) with them. And God's command must be fulfilled."

Some modern Muslim writers have been sweating profusely to explain this issue away. They say it was because Zainab was too proud of her beauty and so the husband was no longer interested in keeping her. An Apostle of Jesus Christ or a Pastor would have taught his converts the Godly principles of a successful marriage instead of taking over the wife (Ephesians 5:22-33; Colossians 3:18-19). Some apologists tell us that Zaid willingly divorced Zainab and gave her to the Prophet on his own volition and with all his heart; and that according to the Quran itself, Zaid had no more desire to keep her.

We all know that this could hardly be true. Zaid could hardly have willingly, with all his heart, relinquished his newly wedded darling to somebody else. Neither could Zainab have *willingly* abandoned her youthful, energetic, vibrant husband for an over 50-year old. But the young couple had no choice in this matter. Zaid was being respectful. He did not want to show his disappointment and sadness about the behaviour of his father — a man who had been so nice to him since childhood. Moreover, since Mohammed had insisted that his claim over Zaid's wife was the will and decree of Allah, there was nothing Zaid could do but submit. That is what makes a good Muslim: submission to the will of Allah. The prophet Mohammed has issued a warning on anybody's reaction on this matter. He said, "It is not fitting for a Believer, man or woman, when a matter has been decided by God and His apostle, to have any option about their decision: If anyone disobeys God and His Apostle, he is indeed on a clearly wrong Path." (Surah 33:36. Read also Sahih al-Bukhari, Hadith No.384, Vol.9).

Did Mohammed actually have such a revelation as here recorded in the Quran? Muslims say, yes. Was it from Allah? They say, yes. One wonders then who this Allah is that makes such a commandment and "turneth the hearts of men" to do such a thing.

King David of Israel fell into an almost similar temptation. But he never justified his action; and God never condoned it. He was punished for it. In the revelation that came to him through Nathan the Prophet, God said: *"Now therefore the sword shall never depart from thine house; because thou hast despised me, and hast taken the wife of Uriah the Hittite to be thy wife."* (2 Samuel 12:10). The sword has still not departed from the house of David today! God is saying here that by taking Uriah's wife David was despising Him who has given every man his own wife. That is why we do not believe that the same God speaking in the Bible could lead Mohammed to take somebody else's wife — the wife of his own adopted son.

Apart from the four wives that Muslims are allowed to have, Allah says in Surah 4:24ff that they are free to take their slave girls as wives. If he is a traveller, a tourist or a pilgrim, the faithful Muslim may have some other temporary 'wives' at strategic places wherever he lodges. This 'marriage' is what is known as *mut'a* or the Law of Desire ('mut'a' means 'Desire'). It may last for an hour or as long as the man desires. Iran is regarded as an example of the kingdom of Allah on earth, and according to a research work by an Iranian woman, Shahla Haeri, *mut'a* flourishes there today.[1] Historian Burkhardt has pointed out that *mut'a* was already prevalent in Arabia before Mohammed started his preaching. The custom was that a host would normally offer a female relative of his to his guest for the night. The 'marriage' ended the following morning or as long as the guest stayed there. If Allah approved this kind of practice even if with some amendments as claimed by the Muslims who practise *mut'a*, our dictionaries may have to redefine adultery and fornication. The Biblical definitions and standard remain unchangeable, however (2 Timothy 2:19).

When every year foreign journalists complain of prostitution in Mecca during the Hajj, it is because they do not understand the divine backing of what goes on. To the Christian, all this automatically violates God's clear injunction: *"Thou shalt not commit adultery."* To a Muslim, such a commandment is vague.

And if you are a young woman, engaged to marry a Muslim, take note. As a husband, your man has permission from Allah in Surah 4:34 to beat you up anytime you misbehave. As an alternative he may refuse to move close to you for a long time as a punishment, since he has others inside or outside. But compare this with what the God of the Bible commands the husband-wife relationship to be in Ephesians 5:25-33, Colossians 3:19, 1 Corinthians 7:2-5.

With this background of the marital life in Islam, it is perhaps not surprising that the Islamic heaven should be full of 'women affairs' as seen earlier. But apart from the unlimited honeymoons of Mohammed's

1 Haeri, Shahla: Law of Desire, I.B Tauris & Co., Ltd., 110 Gloucester Avenue, London NW1 8JA, (1989), p.1

paradise, there are also "rivers of wine" flowing in that heaven! (Surah 47:15; Surah 76:5,21; Surah 83:25-29). In Surahs 5:93 and 2:219, wine is forbidden. Some have seen this as a contradiction. But we do not have to regard it so. Abstinence here may simply be to prepare our throats for the Great Beyond. In fact, one Hadith says, "He who drinks wine in this world and dies when he is addicted to it, not having repented, will not drink it in the next." (Mishkat al Masabih, Sh. M. Ashraf, Lahore 1990, p. 776).

With all the drinking sprees and women affairs in the Islamic heaven, observers have wondered if Allah would not have a problem getting the attention of Muslims to worship him in that Paradise. Someone asks, 'Will all these orgies and this profligacy be enjoyed right in the presence of God in Heaven?' The fact is that in the Muslim heaven God is not even present. We have not seen a description of heaven in the whole Quran showing evidence of God being present there. There is no worship of God there. They have done enough worship on earth.

Now, it is time for sensuous enjoyment unlimited. So, does a Muslim who lived on earth worshipping a God he did not know go to a heaven where he still will not know or see that God or His glory?

Of course, man will be able to see God. Jesus said, *"Blessed are the pure in heart, for they shall see God."* (Matthew 5:8). If anyone dies in his sins without being forgiven here on earth before death, no matter what religion he had on earth, he will not go to Heaven, but will be consigned to Hell.

Jesus told a certain very religious woman, *"Ye (Samaritans) worship ye know not what: we know what we worship: for salvation is of the Jews."* (John 4:22). To those who believe in Him, the Lord said: *"Let not your heart be troubled: ye believe in God, believe also in me. In my Father's house are many mansions: if it were not so, I would have told you. I go to prepare a place for you. And if I go and prepare a place for you, I will come again, and receive you unto myself; that where I am, there ye may be also. And whither I go ye know, and the way ye know. Thomas saith unto him, Lord, we know not whither thou goest; and how can we know the way? Jesus saith unto him, I am the way, the truth, and the life: no man cometh unto the Father, but by me."* (John 14:1-6).

So, the Heaven of the Christian is where Jesus is. They will see Him with the Father in glory. The Bible says, *"...we shall see him as he is."* (1 John 3:2; Revelation 22:3-4).

The 'rivers of wine' issue has been an embarrassment to a few thoughtful Muslim exegetes. But they are smart guys! Some of them, in an attempt to explain this away, say that the wine is not actually alcoholic, (for they could not imagine how such a heaven could be). But one of them goes on to explain that even if the rivers are really alcoholic, that would even be the very reason a committed Muslim should not take wine or beer here on earth, since there would be enough of that in their heaven.

But the Bible says: *"For this ye know, that no whoremonger, nor unclean person, nor covetous man, who is an idolater, hath any inheritance in the kingdom of Christ and of God. Let no man deceive you with vain words: for because of these things cometh the wrath of God upon the children of disobedience. Be not ye therefore partakers with them."* (Ephesians 5:5-7).

"Now the works (practices) *of the flesh are manifest, which are these; Adultery, fornication, uncleanness, lasciviousness, Idolatry, witchcraft, hatred, variance, emulations, wrath, strife, seditions, heresies, Envyings, murders, drunkenness, revellings, and such like: of the which I tell you before, as I have also told you in time past, that they which do such things shall NOT inherit the Kingdom of God."* (Galatians 5:19-21).

The joy of the Christian heaven is not in drinking and in sex. *"For the kingdom of God is not meat and drink; but righteousness, and peace, and joy in the Holy Ghost."* (Romans 14:17). Surely, there is going to be one particular occasion during the 'Marriage Supper of the Lamb', when Jesus will come together with all His people to share the juice of the fruit of the vine as one of the things to enjoy (Matthew 26:26-29). It is the common grape or vine juice He produced during the Marriage at Cana in Galilee, and the one He took with bread during the Last Supper with the disciples. It is the common health drink of the Jews (1 Timothy 5:23).

But certainly there is nothing like "rivers of wine" in Jesus' heaven. What he promises is the 'water of life', and what John saw in his revelation is 'springs of living water' (Revelation 21:6-8; 22:1-2). And we can be sure 'living water' does not mean wine or liquor. The Christian heaven is more wonderful than we can imagine. While wine and women may be the most exciting and thrilling things Mohammed could imagine, the experiences of the redeemed of the Lord will far exceed them. The joy of heaven is not of the earth, and so there can be no human expressions that can adequately describe it. The Bible says, *"But as it is written, Eye hath not seen, nor ear heard, neither have entered into the heart of man, the things which God hath prepared for them that love Him."* (1 Corinthians 2:9).

John saw only a glimpse of it in Revelation and could describe only as far as he could as a human being. In Matthew 22:30, Jesus says the very opposite of what Mohammed says about heaven. We may ask if this Allah who 'revealed' the doctrine to Mohammed is the same God from whom Jesus said He received His messages. Jesus said, *"I have not spoken of myself, but the Father which sent me..., whatsoever I speak therefore, even as the Father said unto me, so I speak."* (John 12:49-50).

Who is the Father?

What About The Marriage Of The Lamb?

The Bible indeed talks of The Marriage Supper of the Lamb that will take place in heaven. (Revelation 19:7-9). This event has nothing to do with the sex-acts of the Mohammedan paradise or 'Gardens of Retreat'. The Marriage of the Lamb is not between individuals. It is the joining of the Lord Jesus Christ, the Lamb of God, and His Church.

The Church of God which is the body of all who have been 'called out' of the world to reign with Him, is often referred to in Scripture as 'the Bride'. The metaphor of Bride-Bridegroom is used to show the preciousness of the Church of Christ, His love for 'her', how He cherishes 'her', and the preparations being made by Him to receive 'her' into glory into "my Father's house" (Ephesians 5:25-32). But Allah says, "We shall espouse them to wide-eyed houris" (Surah 44:54; Surah 52:20; Surah 56:20, A.J.Arberry).

As for those who believe in these heavenly weddings, Jesus says, *"Ye do err, not knowing the Scriptures, nor the power of God. For in the resurrection they neither marry, nor are given in marriage, but are as the angels of God in heaven."* (Matthew 22:29-30, Mark 12:24-25).

Muslim historians have pointed out that life in pre-Islamic Arabia was a life of "the three w's" — wine, women and war.[2] It is therefore not surprising that the new religion should be preferable to the Gospel of Christ. Here they could wage war to even gain paradise; they could have many women especially as the booty of war; and they could expect more women and more free wine when they died. Who would not opt for that?

---

2 Khan, M. Ebrahim; 'Anecdotes from Islam' Sh. Muhammad Ashraf, Lahore (1960) p.13

CHAPTER SEVEN
Allah Can Mislead To Hell?

THERE are several verses in the Quran which state that Allah can decide to mislead a person from the way of salvation if he chooses to (Surahs 16:93; 13:27; 25:9). While Surah 4:88 warns that nobody should lead a person who has been led astray by Allah to the way of salvation, it queries: "Wish you to guide him whom Allah has made to go astray? He whom Allah has made go astray, you will never find for him any way (of guidance)." In Surah 74:31, we learn that "Allah leads astray whom He will and guides whom He will." In Surah 14:4, we read, "Allah misleads whom He will and guides whom He will. He is the All-Mighty, the All-Wise." (All quotes here from Dr M.T. Al-Hilali and Dr Muhsin Khan's translation).

I am personally glad, however, that Allah cannot mislead me because he is not my guide. It is only those who listen to him, those who follow his words, those whom he leads, that he can mislead. Jesus said, *"..I am the light of the world: he that followeth me shall not walk in darkness, but shall have the light of life."* (John 8:12). The God and Father of our Lord Jesus Christ is the One we Christians follow, and we can never be led astray to Hell by that God. The God of the Bible is a God *"Who will have all men to be saved, and to come into the knowledge of the truth."* (1 Timothy 2:4; 2 Peter 3:9). That is why He provides opportunities to discover the truth. He is a God who started the plan of salvation of man on earth since the very day man sinned and fell (Genesis 3:7, 21). An Allah that arbitrarily leads man to hell fire cannot be that Lord.

In Surah 7:179, Allah says, "Many are the Jinns and men we have made for Hell". That is, there are many people that have been created with the purpose of just spending some time here on earth and thereafter to be herded into Hell. But we understand from the Bible that the good God did not make any human being for Hell; neither did He even create Hell for man. Jesus said Hell was created for Satan and his angels (Matthew 25:41). Many people will be in Hell not because the place was made for them, but because they followed Satan and his demonic teachings. If you follow anyone, both of you will find yourselves heading to the same destination. That is the case of the human beings who will find themselves in Hell. Even the evil spirits that will be turned to Hell were not created originally for the purpose of Hell. It was when they sinned that God must have created Hell. The Bible says *In the beginning, God created the heaven* (the firmament and the planets) *and the earth*". It is the devil that rebelled against God and made many other Jinns rebel with him so that they will all be in Hell together. It was he that also tempted mankind and continues to lead man into sin, false religions and all sorts of wickedness today, in order to make them accompany him to Hell. So, when we read, "Many are the Jinns and men we have made for Hell", it is easy for us to recognise that this is not the voice of the God of the Bible.

All Muslims Will Go To Hell?

The Quran makes a shocking but clear statement that apart from 'unbelievers', ALL Muslims will go to hell, first, before being rescued, while the kafirun (unbelievers) would remain there: "There is not one of you but will pass over it (hell), this is with your Lord, a Decree which must be accomplished. But we shall save those who were righteous and we shall leave the wrong-doers therein (humbled) to their knees" (Surah 19:71-72).

In case of any doubt about the meaning or correct rendering of these verses, especially verse 71, let me quote N.J. Dawood's translation (*Koran*, Penguin Books Ltd., 1959): "There is not one of you who shall not pass through the confines of hell..."[1]

J.M. Rodwell's translation (1950 edition) renders it: "No one there is of you who shall not go down into it..."

The popular Mohammed Marmaduke Pickthall's translation, (*The Meaning of the Glorious Koran*, New York, 1954) puts the three verses this way: "There is not one of you but shall approach it. That is a fixed ordinance of thy Lord. Then we shall rescue those who are kept from evil, and leave the evildoers crouching there."

In a later edition, Pickthall recasts the second sentence as: "That is a fixed decree of thy Lord."

Professor A.J. Arberry's translation has it as: "We shall parade them about Gehenna (Hell Fire) hobbling on their knees. Then We shall pluck forth from every party whichever of them was the most hardened...then We shall know very well those most deserving to burn there. Not one of you there is, but he shall go down to it; that for thy Lord is a thing decreed, determined. Then We shall deliver those that were godfearing; and the evildoers We shall leave there, hobbling on their knees." (from verse 69).

Commenting on Surah 42:13, Drs Muhammad Al-Hilali and Muhsin Khan quote Mohammed as saying "Jews will be divided into 71 religious sects and the Christians will be divided into 72 religious sects and this nation (Muslims) will be divided into 73 religious sects — all in Hell, except one". It is in this context that we can understand Surah 19:68-69, "...We shall gather them (all these people) together

1 This has been changed to '...pass through it' in the 1990 revision

95

and also the devils (with them); then We shall bring them round Hell on their knees. Then indeed we shall drag out from every sect all those who were worst in obstinate rebellion against the Beneficient (Allah)" (Al-Hilali & Khan translation).

If words have meaning for you, then what Allah is revealing to you (if you are a Muslim) is that as a matter of the policy of Allah, 'thy Lord', being a Muslim is sufficient to qualify you as a candidate of hell in the first place; and that your 'salvation' would come only when you are already in hell. This may sound strange, but there is an amount of truth in it. The only thing that is wrong there is that you cannot be rescued from the power of hell once you are in. *"But Abraham said...between us and you there is a great gulf fixed: so that they which would pass from hence to you cannot; neither can they pass to us, that would come from thence."* (Luke 16:25,26). *"For if the word spoken by angels was steadfast, and every transgression and disobedience received a just recompence of reward; how shall we escape, if we neglect so great salvation..."* offered in Jesus? (Hebrews 2:2-3).

Compare Allah's way of 'salvation' with that offered by Jesus Christ in the gospel: *"There is therefore now no condemnation to them which are in Christ Jesus..."* (Romans 8:1).

Do we need to go to hell before we are saved from it, before we are 'plucked forth'?

"In fact, it seems Mohammed himself did not know for sure whether or not he was one of those in the sects (party) that will be "plucked forth" from Hell or will remain there. This is because in the Hadith, it is reported: "I heard the Messenger of Allah say — Verily the Almighty and Glorious Allah caught one party with His right hand and another with another hand, and said "This is for this, and this is for this, and I don't care. I don't know in which of the two parties I am" [Mishkat al Masabih, Vol. 3, Chapt. 33:32 (455W), cited in Gerhard Nehls, *Destination Unknown*, Life Challenge, Nairobi (1992) p.3]. What that means is that Allah has already divided man into two parties — the group destined for Heaven, and that of those destined for Hell; and here the prophet of Islam is quoted as saying he does not actually know himself which group he belongs to. Again in Surah 46:9, Allah tells Mohammed, "Say: I am no bringer of new-fangled doctrine among the apostles, **nor do I know what will be done with me or with you**. I follow but that which is revealed to me by inspiration; I am but a warner open and clear".

The Bible calls Jesus a Rock in Zion, a Stone, a tried Stone, *"Whosoever believeth on him shall not be ashamed."* (Romans 10:11). *"...and that Rock was Christ."* (1 Corinthians 10:4). Wise men build their faith on the Rock and they are saved as well as safe. Muslims have built their faith on some unreliable 'five pillars'. Many will discover immediately they die that they have been deceived, and there will be no remedy for them at that time. Their 'pillars' will crumble in the face of the reality of eternal sufferings in hell. God is calling every Muslim reading this book to think again about the true nature of his religion. Remember you are accountable to God as an individual for whatever opportunity you have on earth to be saved from deception.

"Have not I held my peace even of old, and thou fearest me not?" *"for ye compass sea and land to make one proselyte, and when he is made, ye make him twofold more the child of hell than yourselves,"* *"If therefore the light that is in thee be darkness, how great is that darkness!"* (Isaiah 57:11; Matthew 23:15; Matthew 6:23).

If you are a Muslim, think now about what will become of your soul when after all your zeal and sincerity you discover in the end you have missed it.

A Pastor was right to observe that not all Muslims are what they pretend to be. Maybe you, my reader, are one such person. Maybe you would want to love God; maybe you would serve the true God with all your heart if you knew the truth. Maybe you could not help it because you were born into it; maybe you have gone very deep and become popular in Islam, but do not want to experience what men would say about you if you are born again into God's real family of love, joy, peace and eternal life. Maybe you do not personally want to hate Christians but there is something inside you that normally incites you against them, and you want to be free from that something — that spirit of hatred. God says *"Whosoever hateth his brother is a murderer; and ye know that no murderer hath eternal life."* (1 John 3:15). But you don't want to continue bearing that name — being under a judgment as a murderer. You want to empty yourself of all bitterness against the Lord Jesus and His people, and receive Him into your own life too.

God is ready to receive you. No matter how far you have gone, He can completely forgive you and give you a new life from this moment if you mean business. It is real. The Holy Spirit is beside you now to see your reaction to what you are reading here.

What should be really important to you is not to have a popular religion, but to have salvation. If that is the case, you can bow your head or kneel down now, to say that you are sorry for your past life, and ask God to wash your sins away by the blood of Jesus. If you do so wholeheartedly, a heavy burden will be lifted off you, and you can be sure God has given you a new birth. Pray now in your own words.

Allah And The Hope Of Sinners

A sinner who is sincerely seeking for a sure and certain hope of salvation and rest for his soul and takes the Quran to read, if he has any sense of logic, will be totally disappointed. According to the Quran, Allah has no plan, burden or concern to save anybody who does not already believe. In fact, Allah has already decided not to save some people. "As to those who reject the Faith, it is the same to them whether thou warn them or do not warn them: They will not believe. God hath set a seal on their hearts and on their hearing, and on their eyes is a veil; Great is the penalty they (incur)." (Surah 2:6-7).

"God loveth not those who reject Faith" (Surah 3:32).

"God loveth not transgressors" (Surah 2:190, 276; Surah 3:140; Surah 6:141; Surah 42:40).

This is repeated in several other places in the Quran and we need not list all.

If Allah does not love sinners, who are the people he loves?

Only those who love him (Surah 3:31; Surah 5:57).

He loves those who fight wars in order to spread Islam (Surah 61:4).

He loves the just, the righteous, the kind, those who do good and are neat and clean (Surahs 5:14, 45; 49:9; 60:8; 2:222; 9:108).

It is not easy to understand who this Allah is. "God has pre-ordained five things for every man He has created: his period of life, his action, his lying down, his moving about, and his provision" [Mishkat al Masabih, Sh. M. Ashraf (1990) p.30].

Allah does not love the impatient; but he has created man impatient (Surah 70:19).

Allah does not love the niggardly; but he has created all men niggardly (Surah 70:21; Surah 17:100).

Allah does not love those who exult in riches (Surah 28:76). Yet Allah has created every man "violent in his love of wealth" (Surah 100:8). If this is the case, in what position do the arab kings and princes stand before Allah?

There is no clear-cut principle of justice by which the Allah of the Quran will judge Muslims. He says, "And had Allah willed, He could have made you (all) one nation but He sends whom He will astray and guides whom He will, but you shall certainly be asked for what you used to do."(Surah 16:93 Al Hilali et al.). That is, if you sin, Allah must have led you to do it. Yet he will throw you to hell when you die!

In the Hadith, Mohammed is quoted as saying, "Verily Allah has fixed the very portion of adultery which a man will indulge in, and which he of necessity must commit."[2]

If you are a Muslim, don't tell me you are confused. That is what your holy book says — and there are lots more if you want us to go further! If you doubt these quotes, or think we are quoting out of context, take out your Quran and check them patiently, up and down. (See notes on page 4.)

Now, if those are the people Allah hates, and those He loves, who then can be saved through Islam? Go over these verses again and reflect. We all know the Bible is true when it declares, *"For all have sinned, and come short of the glory of God."* (Romans 3:23).

But the message of the Gospel (good news) of Jesus Christ is that *"For God so loved the world, (sinners) that he gave his only begotten Son, that whosoever believeth in Him* **should not perish,** *but have everlasting life. For God sent not his Son into the world to condemn the world; but that the world through him might be saved. He that believeth on him is* **not condemned** *.."*. (John 3:16-18).

---

2 Sahih Muslim, Sh. Muhammad Ashraf, Lahore (1975) Vol.iv pp.1396-8. This is also found in Mishkat al Masabih, Vol.3, Chp 32:6 as reported by Abu Huraira.

The God of the Bible does not love us because we are good. He loves us despite our sins, and therefore made provision to save us from our sins and to forgive us of those we have committed. We have no merit for what God has done for us. The Bible says: *"But God commendeth* (demonstrates) *his love toward us, in that, while we were yet sinners, Christ died for us."* (Romans 5:8).

Jesus Himself said: *"Greater love hath no man than this, that a man lay down his life for his friends."* (John 15:13).

We call on anyone, any sinner, any Muslim who needs love, truth and a reliable plan of salvation to consider the God of the Bible and compare Him with whatever god he already believes in.

Each chapter of the Quran begins with the statement: "In the name of Allah, the most compassionate and merciful." But ask the Muslim what Allah has done about his sins. He has no specific answer. "Maybe God will forgive me, maybe He will not. Until I get to heaven when my good works will be weighed on a scale against my evil works...".

Grace means an unmerited or undeserved favour. But where is the mercy of God if He did not give us a definite and sure way for salvation of our souls? Where is the grace if He expects us to struggle and earn earn salvation by our own efforts, when He knows full well our frailty and weaknesses as human beings who are 'only evil continually'? Is Allah's compassion and mercy only in giving Muslims daily food and four wives?

If God would judge us on the basis of our personal struggles, it means His compassion does not go beyond the grave. But the Christian's belief about God's compassion is that because He understands man's frailty and the high demand of His own law and sees man's inability to fulfil the law, He came down to fulfil the law in a Person (Matthew 5:17). All the punishment a sinner deserves is met in that person, so that *"by the obedience of One, shall many be made righteous"* (Romans 5:19). All God now says is that man should believe this simply and accept the offer. That is how the Christian believes God to be most compassionate and merciful.

We do not find it easy to believe that Allah could be 'most merciful' and yet determine to "fill the hell with mankind and jinns together" as a "fixed ordinance".

The Christian Bible says *"O give thanks unto the* LORD; *for he is good: for his mercy endureth for ever."* (Psalm 106:1).That His mercy endures for ever means that it is eternal. And if it is eternal, that means that it goes beyond the grave; and if His mercy does go beyond the grave, that means it must cover the consequences of our sins that might otherwise be waiting for us beyond the grave. The Christian faith is positive and not fatalistic. The Christian believes the compassion of God is embodied in Jesus Christ, and so anyone who has Jesus has all the fullness of God's love.

As a Muslim, whenever you say that Allah is 'most merciful, most compassionate and gracious', ask yourself immediately, 'what definite thing has this Allah done concerning my sins?'

Allah And The Washing Away Of The Sinner's Sin

The Quran says, "O ye who believe! When ye prepare for prayer, wash your faces, and your hands (and arms) to the elbows; Rub your heads (with water); and (wash) your feet to the ankles" (Surah 5:7). This is what is called Ablution (wud'u). The purpose of this is to make the Muslim pure in the sight of Allah when praying. Surah 5:7 and 4:43 say if Muslims do not have water around (e.g. a traveller), they should take for themselves clean sand or earth, and rub therewith their faces and hands. "For God doth blot out sins and forgive again and again". A former devoted Muslim told me that he now feels annoyed with himself as even though he was a respectable Chartered Accountant, he still had to rub his face with sand when he was a Muslim because of his love for Islam. Even though he is no longer a Muslim, he still feels annoyed that he ever did such a thing!

The speaker in the Quran does not seem to have the right perspective of sin; neither does he know or at least want us to know how serious sin can be in the sight of a holy God. This is evident in the suggestion that the washing of teeth, nose, ears and limbs by water or sand can change a man's sinful nature and wash away his personal wicked acts to be able to stand before a holy God. The Psalmist says: *"Who shall ascend into the hill of the LORD? or who shall stand in his holy place? He that hath clean hands and a pure heart..."* (Psalm 24:3-4).

No, the 'clean hands' here does not mean hands washed with water. What makes a hand unclean is what one does with the hand — charms, tiras, mascots, killings, sponsoring of evil works, destruction of houses and churches, taking vengeance, etc. — and not physical dirt. God Himself makes this clear in the book of Jeremiah when He says: *"For though thou wash thee with nitre, and take thee much soap, yet thine iniquity is marked before me, saith the LORD God."* (Jeremiah 2:22).

"For your hands are defiled with blood, and your fingers with iniquity; your lips have spoken lies, your tongue hath muttered perverseness. None calleth for justice, nor any pleadeth for truth: they trust in vanity, and speak lies; they conceive mischief, and bring forth iniquity. They hatch cockatrice' eggs, and weave the spider's web: he that eateth of their eggs dieth, and that which is crushed breaketh out into a viper. Their webs shall not become garments, neither shall they

cover themselves with their works: their works are works of iniquity, and the act of violence is in their hands. Their feet run to evil, and they make haste to shed innocent blood: their thoughts are thoughts of iniquity; wasting and destruction are in their paths. The way of peace they know not; and there is no judgment in their goings: they have made them crooked paths: whosoever goeth therein shall not know peace." (Isaiah 59:3-8).

A bath in the Zamzam well in Mecca cannot cleanse them; no, not even a billion barrels of Arabian perfume can sweeten their hands stained with the blood of people they have slaughtered or sponsored to slaughter. Some of them may not participate in violence, but they morally support those who do. The blood of the children of God not only remains on the hands of all their enemies, but also cries to God daily, saying, "How long, O Lord, holy and true, dost thou not judge and avenge our blood on them..?" (Revelation 6:10; Deuteronomy 32:43).

With this daily crying of the blood of the martyrs of God for vengeance, how does any Muslim think he can escape the judgment of God by daily ablution? The Bible offers a better and surer solution: *"The blood of Jesus Christ his Son cleanseth us from all sin."* (1 John 1:7).

The question of sin and redemption should be the central issue in any true religion; but the devil is capable of creating a religion without a redeemer. Yes, he is capable of creating a worship without a washing away of sin. And here we see an Allah offering a religion without redemption! We have not found any definite plan of salvation in the Quran. 'Jahaanan' (Greek: Gehena) or Hell appears 77 times in the Quran, and there are six other references using different words, making 83 references to Hell. But Paradise is mentioned by name only four times in the whole Quran! All we hear is "Gardens" of pleasure. Think about that.

CHAPTER EIGHT

Islam, The Religion Of Adam

FROM deep Islamic teaching, the religion of Islam did not begin with Mohammed. Muslims claim that it was the religion of Adam, Noah, Ishmael, and all the prophets of God, including Jesus Christ before His crucifixion. The Quran itself says so. For want of space, we examine Islam's identification with only two of these, namely, as it concerns Adam and Jesus Christ.

What we know about Adam is that he was the first man. God did not give him a religion and he was not a prophet. God only asked him to tend the garden of Eden and eat all the fruits there except one. That was all. There is no religion in that. He was given only one commandment. But no sooner did he receive it than he disobeyed it by listening to the voice of someone else who promised that he and his wife would be 'like God' — the very thing that this being aspired to be and the very reason why he, Satan, the serpent or dragon, lost his position in heaven (Isaiah 14:12-15). Adam, on the advice of this crafty being, ate the fruit of knowledge of good and evil and ignored his real personal relationship with God. God drove him from Eden, and he spent most of his life **outside Eden**. If he ever practised any religion at all it must have been done outside the garden of Eden.

If Islam is the religion of Adam, then something should be suspect about it. The religion of Adam as we know it is a religion of disobedience and rebellion against the word of God — a religion practised in his fallen state, outside the Garden of God, outside the Kingdom of God, outside the presence of God; a religion without the opportunity of taking of the fruit of the tree of life. Surely, this cannot be the best religion. Jesus said: *"To him that overcometh will I give to eat of the tree of life, which is in the midst of the* paradise of *God.*" (Revelation 2:7). That is, to him who can overcome the temptations of the devil. Since Adam did not overcome; — to him who succeeds in rejecting the ways of Adam.

With his newly acquired 'knowledge of good and evil', Adam sewed fig leaves to cover his nakedness (sin). But every descendant of Adam and Eve became so depraved that the fruit of knowledge of good and evil notwithstanding, ".*every imagination of the thoughts of his heart was only evil continually.*" (Genesis 6:5). All the good in him, all the righteousness he invented, are, in the sight of a holy God, *"as filthy rags"* (Isaiah 64:6).

Self righteousness. Yes. That is the other religion of Adam, apart from disobedience. When Adam disobeyed God, he knew he had sinned and was eternally separated from the life of God. But he felt he could cover the shame of his sin with fig leaves. God showed that he was foolish, and clothed him with *"coats of skins"* (Genesis 3:21).

Here we note that an animal had to be killed by God before Adam could be properly covered — an innocent animal, possibly a lamb, for its skin is more beautiful for covering than that of other animals.

In the New Testament, we read, *"For Christ also hath once suffered for sins, the just for the unjust"*, *"For he hath made him to be sin for us, who knew no sin; that we might be made the righteousness of God in him."* (1 Peter 3:18; 2 Corinthians 5:21).

The religion inherited from Adam, then, is to try to create a way of clothing oneself with man-made works of righteousness. But the good news is that God has a better way of covering man's sins. And we wish to say that any religion outside the redemptive work of Christ, any religion that ignores the atonement (covering) by God through Jesus, is a fig-leaf religion.

106

David says, *"Blessed is he whose transgression is forgiven, whose sin is covered."* (Psalm 32:1). The 'covering' is done by God Himself and not man. John the Baptist saw Jesus and prophetically declared: *"Behold, the Lamb of God which taketh away the sin of the world."* (John 1:29).

We know man is a sinner because he sins. But conversely, he sins because he is a sinner! Every man came from Adam. If Adam had died at the age of, say six months without an offspring, we would all have died in him. We would not be here today. This means we were in Adam when he was sinning. We became small Adams, small sinners, small rebels.

Therefore, man is a sinner even if he were cultured and hatched in a test-tube! The egg is a sinner; the fertilizer is a sinner. They both have the genes or the potential of a wicked man (Psalm 58:3; 51:5). Man's condition is worsened especially if he finds a god that approves of his wickedness and promises some sensuous heaven as a reward for this.

Therefore, two things have to happen to a man before he can be right with the God of the Bible. First, his past sins, definite acts, have to be forgiven. This is the work of the Blood of Jesus. Secondly, sin itself, that is, the nature that makes a person to sin — the Adamic chromosome — has to be crucified. This is done by the Cross (Ephesians 2:14-16; Galatians 2:20). By that, not only *"old things are passed away"*, but also *"all things are become new."* (2 Corinthians 5:17). Man cannot remain in Adam and please God. All Adamites have always been adamant to the Law of God. And that is why every man has to receive a new life before he can please God.

Now, if Muslims maintain that the religion of Adam was Islam, then we would do well to probe the giver of that religion. Islam means submission, and Adam, indeed submitted. But he did not submit to the real God Almighty. Scripture tells us to whom he submitted and obeyed — the devil. If the one Adam submitted to is the same Allah of Mohammed, what then are Muslims suggesting?

Another doctrine to examine in this regard is the claim by Muslims that even Jesus Christ practised Islam before His crucifixion and that it was after His death that people invented what they now call Christianity. This argument does not hold water. All the claims of Jesus when He was on earth — about Himself, about God, and about the way of salvation — contradict all the basic teachings of Islam. And that explains why serious Muslims reject the Bible and cling to the so-called Gospel of Barnabas.

Mohammed consistently claimed that he brought no new religion or revelation other than the one Jesus brought, and Muslims claim they respect Jesus. Yet many of us know by experience that Islam is the most anti-Christian religion on earth. It is more antagonistic to the Christian faith than Communism ever was. And by this, we do not mean nominal Islam. With all the persecutions Christians suffered in the former Soviet Union, the Church of Christ still continued, though underground. In Communist China today, Christianity still thrives. But confession of Christ by a national in an Islamic country is regarded as high treason. No Church is allowed, not even an official Church that a Communist government could allow, is permitted to operate openly in an Islamic country.

Apart from the fact that Jesus' teachings contradict Mohammed's Quran, Christ could not be said to have a religion in the real sense of the word, nor did He come to establish one. What he brought is redemption and reconciliation — bringing to those who will accept Him a Father-children relationship to God. He did not come to prescribe a uniform system of worship. When a man is in the right relationship with God, he will have the freedom to worship Him and express himself in the best way he can. Religion is an attempt by man to save himself; redemption is God's way to save man: *"God was in Christ, reconciling the world unto himself"* (2 Corinthians 5:19). That is God operating there, not man.

Jesus lived the life of God and imparted this life into all those who believed in Him. After His resurrection, *"he breathed on them,* (disciples) *and saith unto them, Receive ye the Holy Ghost."* (John 20:22). This is the Spirit that sealed the adoption of these disciples as children of God, and it is that Spirit that was bearing witness with their heart that they were the sons of God.

Talking of this Spirit of adoption, the apostle Paul said *"if any man have not the Spirit of Christ, he is none of his,"* (Romans 8:9) — even if he has a popular religion! *"But as many as received him, to them gave he power* (privilege, right, authority) *to become the sons of God"* (John 1:12; 2 Corinthians 1:22).

That is what Christianity is all about; it is possessing and living the life of Christ, in the power of the Holy Spirit; and it is more than religion, even in its most refined form. The Apostle Paul says, *"For we are the circumcision, which worship God in the Spirit, and rejoice in Christ Jesus, and have no confidence in the flesh* (credentials of an outward religion, race and education) *Though I might also have confidence in the flesh. If any other man thinketh that he hath whereof he might trust in the flesh, I more: Circumcised the eighth day, of the stock of Israel, of the tribe of Benjamin, a Hebrew of Hebrews; as touching the law, a Pharisee; Concerning zeal, persecuting the church; touching the righteousness which is in the law, blameless. But what things were gain to me, those I counted loss for Christ. Yea doubtless, and I count all things but loss for the excellency of the knowledge of Christ Jesus my Lord: for whom I have suffered the loss of all things, and do count them but dung, that I may win Christ, And be found in him, not having mine own righteousness, which is of the law, but that which is through the faith of Christ, the righteousness which is of God by faith: That I may know him, and the power of his resurrection, and the fellowship of his sufferings, being made conformable unto his death."* (Philippians 3:3-10).

Here was a man whom, if you like, you might call 'the Chief Imam of Tarsus'. But he soon discovered that it is not by human might in struggling to keep the Law that a man could be saved.

Islam is a religion of law which caters more for the outward appearance, the flesh. But Jesus has come to fulfil the Law in Himself (Matthew 5:17). He, only, has been able to keep the Law, and the whole thing was finished on the Cross. Man has been unable to keep the Law. But Christ has done so, as 'the Son of Man', and the representative of Man. Therefore when a man receives Christ into his life, God clothes that person with His righteousness. God assures us that *"For as many of you as have been baptized into Christ have put on Christ."* (Galatians 3:27). God sees Christians INSIDE Christ, and it is only inside Him that God sees us righteous. God Himself *"Blotting out the handwriting of ordinances that was against us, which was contrary to us, and took it out of the way, nailing it to his cross"* (Colossians 2:14).

Mohammed arose 600 y.ears after the finished work of Christ to exhume another set of laws, which is even inferior to the Jewish Law, and forced people to accept this religion of Law. No one can reject the finished work of Christ and expect to be justified before God by the obeying of some laws (Romans 3:20).

Muslims have succeeded in putting themselves under a curse by choosing a religion of law. The Bible says all who rely on observing the Law are under a curse, *"for it is written, cursed is everyone who continueth not in all things which are written in the book of the law to do them."* (Galatians 3:10; Deuteronomy 27:26).

But as Christians who have accepted the Lordship of Jesus, over our lives, *"Christ hath redeemed us from the curse of the Law..".* (Galatians 3:13). That is the good news called 'the gospel' which Muslims do not want to accept. They do not realise that it is pride in the sight of God to reject God's provision for us and then try to wash our noses, rinse our mouth and kill rams and feel qualified to see the glory of God. The Scripture says, these regulations are all destined to perish with use because they are based on human commands and teachings. Such regulations have an appearance of wisdom, with their self-imposed worship, their false humility and their harsh treatment of the body, but they lack any value in restraining sensual indulgence (Colossians 2:22-23).

That explains why even with four wives, the religious man is still not fulfilled; he has to indulge in concubinage and mut'a. There can be no lasting fulfilment in any area of life unless one experiences the love of God in Christ.

CHAPTER NINE

Authorities Of The Quran And The Bible Re-examined

WE have read several books written by Muslims undermining the authority of the Bible as the Word of God. Publication of such books has been on the increase in the last decade with Ahmed Deedat based in South Africa as a key author. On the other hand, Muslims are usually morbidly afraid of any non-Muslim commenting on the Quran. But for many others who can be patient, and reason, comparing the claims of the Quran and the works of Muslim writers on the Bible, we offer this chapter.

In it we have a very brief examination of the Quran as a religious book, purportedly given by Allah from heaven to his apostle. Many have observed that the Quran is a good attempt to produce a big book for the Muslims, just as the Christians have. It is sufficient to say that it is voluminous because it is a bundle of repetitions. Even if we are expected to regard some aspects of the Quran as inspired by Allah, yet it is obvious that the book is, at best, a glorified package of myths, most of which were taken from the Jewish and Christian Scriptures and traditions and then perverted. The writer of the Quran who did a good job anthologizing apocryphal stories, tautologies, irrelevances and contradictions sufficient to make a big and religious book, should be commended for producing a book as voluminous as four-fifths of the New Testament.

The Bible however, is not the Word of God because it is voluminous. There are much larger books. A billion and one text books have been written ABOUT the Bible — either by believers of the Book or its enemies. Yet nobody has been able to improve upon it, write a better or even similar one. In the providence of God the printing press with movable type was invented at a time when there was a critical need for the circulation of the Scriptures to counter error and spread the Gospel. Despite all attempts by kings of the earth and religious leaders to destroy the Book, pervert its message, or prevent its distribution, it has remained the bestseller of all ages.

As a sinner, I wondered at its probe into my sinful nature. As a believer now, I rejoice at the peace, comfort and assurance of salvation I have in it. As a student, I marvel at the sublimity of the Book, its historicity, its scientificity, and the authority of its tone. In it I see the only hope of a world leading itself to destruction.

It is impossible to fully understand world history and the international scene today without knowing the Bible. Its prophetic authority makes it more relevant than tomorrow's newspapers. The Bible will continue to baffle the ignorant 'learned' heathen until they humble themselves at the feet of the Lord to discover the truth and the life in the Word.

Having rejected the Word of life, man runs about in delusion and depravity of mind seeking for help in such as yoga and all kinds of esoteric cults — even though he pretends he does not believe in the supernatural.

The Bible was written by more than forty different writers from all walks of life — kings (David), princes (Moses), priests (Ezekiel), prophets, politicians and scholars (Ezra, Daniel, Paul), soldiers (Joshua), fishermen (Peter, John), cattle rearers (Amos), tax collectors (Matthew), etc. Most of these people lived years or even centuries apart, many not knowing of each other, nor having met anywhere. Yet the thematic harmony of the whole Book runs through Genesis to Revelation. The writers wrote the same message, yet

113

not one wrote the same way or the same thing as the other. One book finds its complement in the other until there is a consummation of all things in the Book of Revelation. Even the Tree of Life forfeited in Genesis is regained in Revelation.

All this is marvellous in our eyes, and it is sufficient for us to regard it as a book being guided by one Intelligent Mind, the Mind of the Spirit of a faithful and consistent God. Most of those who have accused the Bible of being unscientific and contradictory have begun to swallow their words as they are discovering their own intellectual vacuity — despite their academic titles — and their ignorance of the diction and interpretation of the Scripture. We know that only the uninformed still talk of unscientificity or unhistoricity of the Bible. The King James translation of the Bible is in a peculiarly elegant language with certain elements reminiscent of the age of its translation. But how do we explain the many translations of the Quran written in this 20th century and yet written in some archaic language? Did the scholars think that it is archaism that makes a book divine?

The Bible was written by several people and yet is thematically consistent. The Quran on the other hand, is supposed to have been written by one man, or as Muslims ask us to believe, was written in Heaven by Allah, and yet it surprises us with so many scores of serious categorical contradictions.

It is necessary for us to dig up one or two such contradictions to aid our understanding of who might be speaking in the book. Let us first point out the case of the claim of Mohammed's illiteracy. Some may wonder why great Muslim scholars still maintain the claim of the illiteracy of their prophet and feel no shame about it. There are two reasons for this. First, it is the claim of the Quran itself. The Quran describes Mohammed as al-nabi al-ummi, that is, the unlearned or unlettered prophet (Surah 7:158). Secondly, although some scholars have contended the actual meaning of this verse, such a claim and interpretation by Muslims is necessary to validate the assertion that the Quran was not written by Mohammed but came down from heaven. Since it was given to Mohammed, it is therefore free from human instrumentality.

The cosmogonical and cosmological data in the Quran is in a flux. According to Surah 54:50, the whole Creation was made in the twinkle of an eye. That is, when God spoke his Word of creation, the whole universe came into existence immediately in a split second, that is, in less than one day. Yet Surah 41:9 says the world was created in two days. Verse 10 of the same Surah says four days. Verse 12 says "seven heavens" were created in two days. And again Surah 7:54 says the Creation was made in six days! This is repeated in Surah 10:3 and Surah 32:4. Presumably at that time Mohammed heard of the true Biblical account in Genesis. But he probably forgot to withdraw the former written 'revelations'. And so, during the compilation of the Quran, everything was bound together. But Surah 32:5 also says a day is actually 'a thousand years of your reckoning', thereby compounding our confusion. In Surah 70:4, we read that a day with Allah is not 1,000 years as we have read in the other Surah, but 50,000 years! If Muslims say the Quran was written in heaven and kept by Allah there, we are bound to say that it does not appeal to our human reason ing, and we would prefer a more consistent book.

This book will not make an exhaustive examination of the contradictions. But we need to look at one or two more. These have to do with the statements about Christianity. It is interesting to note that with so much animosity towards everything Christian, there are still places in the Quran with some revealing truths. Allah is quoted, for instance, as saying that the followers of Jesus Christ shall be exalted above all unbelievers until the Day of Resurrection (Surah 3:55). Again, the Quran talks of the Bible as "the Gospel: therein was guidance and light" (Surah 5:49). It confirms Jesus' virgin birth, and that He was the Word of God, and the Spirit of God who put on the flesh of man, etc. One such verses says *inter alia*: "And (remember) her who guarded her chastity: We breathed into her of Our Spirit, and We made her and her Son a Sign for all peoples." (Surah 21:91).

We may wonder who is speaking here: Allah, or the Christian God? If it is God, it means there was at least one particular time when God had to speak through Mohammed on the deity of Jesus. In that case, Mohammed would have no excuse, no matter what his personal biases and envies might be. But if such basic truths are in the Quran and they were revealed by Allah, why then do many Christians not regard the book as a holy book of God? Our answer is: we do not believe in the book because there are categorical denials of all these truths in the same book, and we believe that a holy book should be consistent, especially when it comes to matters affecting the salvation of man.

Here is another example: Allah is quoted in Surah 3:55 as saying to Jesus: 'O Jesus! I will take thee (or cause you to DIE) and raise thee to Myself". Again in Surah 19.33, Jesus is quoted as saying: "So Peace is on me the day I was born, the day that I **die**, and the day that I shall be **raised up to life** (again)"! (emphasis mine.)

However, in an attempt to explain away the crucifixion of Jesus, Mohammed says later in Surah 4:157-158 that Jesus did not die as was reported, neither was He crucified. Rather, "so it was made to appear to them."

If Mohammed is the one who composed the words in the Quran, here then is a person commenting on an event that happened over five hundred years before he was even born, telling us 'it only appeared so'. It is not easy for us to attribute the writing or inspiration of the Quran to God Almighty. We expect a coherence of thought even for an ordinary human being. How could something said in Surah 3 be categorically denied in Surah 4?

What do we have to say about this? There are only two possibilities here. Firstly, that Mohammed is deliberately trying to deny the death and resurrection of Jesus, because such stories would have serious implications for his other messages. Moreover, such stories would have proved Jesus as having the power over death and therefore qualified to be the Saviour. Secondly, the alternative explanation is if Muslims maintain that Mohammed was really being inspired to say this then the one who inspired him must have been a liar and deceiver, saying he would let Jesus die, and could not do that after all.

If by causing Jesus to die, Allah, if he were God, would do a great thing for mankind, it would be a great disappointment if he could not carry out his original plan. In fact, it would be a weakness on his part if Jesus escaped the Cross which he, Allah, had planned for him for a purpose.

Many Islamic scholars are in confusion about what to believe in the Quran concerning the death and resurrection of Jesus Christ. Commenting on Surah 43:61 which says Jesus is the sign of the hour, Helmut Gatje in his book, *The Qu'ran and its Exegesis*, explains *inter alia*, "(Jesus is 'a sign of the Hour') because he showed through his resurrection from the dead that God has the power to raise the dead (on the Day of Judgment)." (p. 129). He has probably forgotten he believes that Jesus neither died nor was resurrected. Yusuf Ali also is confused here, but he seems a bit more honest in his reasoning on the issue. In Commentary No. 2485, he says, "Christ was not crucified (IV: 157). But those who believe that he never died should ponder over this verse, " (that is Verse 33 of Surah 19).

In a bid to explain these conflicting verses and to deliberately ignore the need for a shedding of blood to save mankind, different Muslim sects have developed different ideas. The Ahmadiyyah sect, holding on the theory of Venturini, says Jesus only fainted on the cross or was at most half dead, and that He regained His consciousness while in the grave and then ran away secretly to India where He lived and died a normal death at a good old age. This is the view held by the popular South African Muslim pamphleteer, Ahmed Deedat, in some of his pamphlets he titled *Resurrection or Resuscitation?*, *Crucifixion or Crucifiction?*, etc.

Some other commentators brought in the idea of machine-god (deux-ex-machina) — a dramatic device whereby a divine intervention is introduced to avert an inevitable but unnecessary tragedy at the end of a play. According to the Muslims who hold this view, God had to circumvent the crucifixion of Jesus by miraculously removing Him from the cross to heaven in a twinkle of an eye and replacing Him with someone whom God made to look exactly like Jesus, and who was eventually crucified in His stead.

But who was this substitute? Opinions also differ on this. The popular consensus is that it must be Judas Iscariot. According to them, therefore, it wasn't Jesus that the soldiers crucified: "It only seemeth so in their eyes."

This 'catching away' theory was actually formulated by Muslims in the Middle Ages and clearly entrenched in the Chapter 112 verse 13-17 of the so-called 'Gospel of Barnabas' written at that time by a former Roman Catholic converted to Islam. This book is popular and highly venerated among Muslims as a good weapon for opposing Christian teachings about Jesus. It is therefore not surprising that it is Muslims that publish this book (especially in Pakistan) and circulate it among themselves.

What the authors of the Quran, *The Gospel of Barnabas*, and Muslim commentators do not understand is that the Cross is not a tragedy. It is a victory over the devil and sin. The devil himself knows this. If he denies it in a book, it is only to deceive. He can never forget what happened that day. During this period, Jesus "...*having spoiled principalities and powers, he made a shew of them openly, triumphing over them in it.*" (*Colossians 2:14-15*).

The Cross was God's formula of 'life through death'. Jesus did not come to establish a worship system. He did not come to give a Law but to give His love. In other words, His law was love.

He came primarily to die, and there was no need for Him to escape it (Matthew 16:21). If God didn't want Jesus to be killed, there would be no need for him to 'steal' Him away. All He would have needed to do would be to send down a few angels to destroy the soldiers and allow Jesus to continue His ministry right there in Jerusalem.[1] 'Stealing' Jesus away would mean showing God's helplessness and defeat by terminating the ministry of Christ prematurely. What some want us to believe is that Jesus was a nice gentleman who preached love and peace, and then somehow events got out of hand and he fell helplessly into the hands of an angry mob.

We know that this is not true. Jesus went to the Cross willingly. He was in absolute control of every event in His life — including the timing! Even on the night of His arrest when Judas, who was to identify

---

1 Jesus Himself hinted at this possibility in Matthew 26:53.

Him, was still delaying going to the chief priests for the deal, the Lord had to hasten him: *"That thou doest, do quickly."* (John 13:27-29). This shows that His arrest must take place that particular night unfailingly, according to His strict time-table. It also shows there was that will in Him to die, and it was never rescinded.

But if Muslims maintain that Jesus never died but was taken up to heaven alive, then they must admit to these logical conclusions: First, Jesus is still alive today just as He was on earth, for we cannot imagine Him dying in heaven. Second, if Jesus has not died, and never will, then the claim of Mohammed as the successor of Jesus is null and void.

If, however, the Quran verses (Surah 3:55 and 19:33) are predictions of Jesus' death when He returns to the earth as some other Muslim exegetes say, then we would still say that until that happens, nobody can succeed Him.

Now, let us examine this: The person Mohammed said he was succeeding is still alive. But Mohammed himself is dead. If what made Mohammed a 'natural successor' was the physical absence of Jesus, what happens now that Mohammed is no more here? Who owns the throne?

The fact is that the Throne has never been vacant at any time because the King is still alive. Genuine prophets of the real God have come and gone forever. The Bible says, *"And they truly were many priests, because they were not suffered to continue by reason of death: But this man, because he continueth ever, has an unchangeable priesthood. Wherefore he is able also to save them to the uttermost that come into God by him, seeing he ever liveth to make intercession for them."* (Hebrews 7:23-25). He intercedes for us; we don't say 'peace be upon him'; He is our peace. He said, *'My peace I give unto you.'* (John 14:27).

Muslims really hate the idea of the resurrection of Jesus. That is why it has become necessary for them to deny His death first. And it is amazing how much effort they have made to twist the translation of these verses to hide the meaning. In Surah 3:55 quoted earlier, for example, Mohammed Marmaduke Pickthall has decided to translate the expression rendered "I will cause you to die" as "I am gathering thee." Going to the original Arabic Quran, the expression here is *Inni muta-waf-feeka*. Sincere Arabs must ask themselves why Pickthall had to translate this as "gathering". Dr Anis Shorrosh said: *"As an Arab, I have never known of any other meaning than death for this expression, within or without the Quran."*[2]

We can understand the reason for Pickthall's translation. The Australian Anti-Communist Crusader, Dr Fred Schwartz, has observed that, 'No matter how clear the evidence is, people can always find an interpretation that will allow them to cling to what they want to believe.' The fact is that the doctrine of the Cross and the consequent Resurrection is offensive to Muslims and they must explain it away.

Commenting on Surah 3:59, A. Yusuf Ali says, "Jesus was as dust just as Adam was or humanity is."[3] Ali is only echoing what the Quran itself says in that verse. Christians take this view by Mohammed in the Quran as blasphemous, because we know Jesus is divine. Those who share this Quranic view with Ali should remember God indeed cursed Adam and humanity to return to dust from which man was created: *"for dust thou art, and unto dust shalt thou return."* (Genesis 3:19). Adam died and his body returned to the dust after decaying. All humanity

2 Shorrosh, A. *"Islam Revealed*', A Christian Arab's View of Islam, Thomas Nelson, Nashville, (1989) p.97
3 Ali, Yusuf *'Qur'an Text', Translation & Commentary'*, Commentary No. 398

is under this curse of putrefaction. Even if a dead body is mummified, the fact that it has no life makes it no more important than the dust. The body is no longer a 'he' but an 'it', and no less an 'it' than the dust! But what if cremated? It is even worse to turn to ashes than to dust!!

Even though Mohammed said he was an ordinary man, and Muslims claim they do not worship him, yet, it is evident the man has been exalted to the level of deity. That is why Muslims often talk of 'blaspheming our prophet'. Muslims do not realise that they commit the unforgivable sin of *shirk* by regarding Mohammed as blasphemable. Only God is divine, and therefore the only One that can be blasphemed! Jesus, as the Son of God, can be blasphemed, and the Holy Spirit of God can be blasphemed because they are God (Acts 5:3-4; John 14:7; John 20:28-29). This many Muslims have done consistently through their writings and preachings which are taken from the Quran itself. As an ordinary human being, Mohammed was also under the curse of dust to dust put on mankind. The dust and the dry bones in his grave in Medina today are proof of this.

But where is the body of Jesus whom Muslims believe was 'as dust just as Adam or humanity'? Where is that dust? Even though many Muslims may deny that Jesus ever died or was resurrected, they all agree, according to their Quran, that Christ was taken up to Heaven, body, soul and spirit. And since He cannot die up there, they must take it, as a logical corollary, that He is still alive today in regal glory, waiting for His Second Coming. It necessarily follows that He is *"the same yesterday, and today, and for ever"*! (Hebrews 13:8).

Now if the body of Jesus defied the curse put on humanity, does this not raise Him above humanity? Yes. And verily, verily we say this unto you: it is because Jesus is above humanity that He is qualified to be the Saviour of the world! Gloire à Dieu!

122

A story has it that when Mohammed died, his people thought that having proclaimed himself 'the seal of the prophets', and therefore the greatest, he would at least rise up, probably on the third day, and ascend to heaven bodily as Jesus did. For this reason, they refused to dig the grave deep, neither did they bury the remains in a coffin so that he would find it easier to come out of the grave. But Death and Grave held him and have not released him. If this story is true, we do not think Muslims should be disappointed that the remains of their prophet decayed and became dust. Allah never promised Mohammed would resurrect like Jesus; so why should they feel disappointed?

But because everything that Mohammed did, or things that were done to him by his disciples as recorded in the Traditions must be copied as examples to follow, it is interesting to note that even till today, Muslims do not dig the ground deep to bury their dead; neither do they normally bury in a coffin. Many of them, though, do not know how these things began. False messiahs may rise and make bogus claims about themselves. But Death usually comes and deals its blow to them and they are consumed in the earth. But the Eternal King of kings Himself, many years after His Resurrection and Ascension, spoke to John: *"I am he that liveth, and was dead; and, behold, I am alive for evermore, Amen; and have the keys of hell and of death."* (Revelation 1:18).

Muslims need to understand that the Cross of Jesus was necessary. *"The wages of sin is **death**,"* (Romans 6:23), and because Jesus was carrying the sin of the whole world on the cross, He was made to DIE! By that, God made *"His soul an offering for sin"* (Isaiah 53:10; 2 Corinthians 5:21). But to give His believers victory over sin, as well as over Satan, demons and the second death, Jesus had to rise again on the third day. Many enemies of the

Gospel today have tried to **deny** these facts, but none of them has been able to **refute** them. All the 'proofs' they have presented only helped to show the futility of their minds and how uninformed they are concerning the historicity of these events. Peter stood in the midst of several thousands of Jews in Jerusalem on the day of Pentecost and spoke of the resurrection of Christ, and what His death and resurrection had done for mankind. No single person among his listeners rose to say Jesus was not killed or resurrected. They all knew this was the talk of the town. Mohammed was born over 500 years later to say that Jesus did not die, and that it was Allah that told him so.

We reject the Quran because it denies history — history recorded not only by Christians but by many secular writers. These commentators of that time lived in the same period of the early Christians, and in the environment of these events, and would have denied the Christians' claims if the claims were untrue. Yes, the Quran has certain truths, but we reject the book because we believe a half-truth is more dangerous than a blatant lie. We know the devil is a liar and the inspirer of all lies. Jesus said when Satan lies, he is not doing anything strange, but: *"When he speaketh a lie, he speaketh of his own: for he is a liar, and the father of it."* (John 8:44).

But it must be realised that Satan is not just a liar but a deceiver! And to be an excellent deceiver, he knows he has to slot in one or two truths into a bundle of lies. That, exactly, is how he is able to deceive many people today in false religions and cults who use some statements in the Bible to establish their cults and destroy themselves.

The fact that there are a few biblically true state-ments in the Quran does not make the book the Word of God. This is a classic diabolical deception.

As Tennyson, the poet, wrote:

"A lie that's a half-truth is the wickedest lie of all,
For a lie that's all a lie can be met with and fought outright
But a lie that is a half-truth is a harder matter to fight."

Yet on the other hand, the presence of some of these truths in the Quran serves as a testimony against all Muslims who reject the gospel of Jesus Christ. We thank God that some of these bits of truth have led some Muslims to inquire more of *Christ in* the Bible and they have thereby found Him as He really is.

In his book, *Buddha, Mohammed and Christ*, Dr Marcus Dodds has observed that Mohammed's book can never be received by serious-minded people as a reliable authority on the gospel of Jesus nor as a history book on the heroes of the Bible: "His (Mohammed's) knowledge of Christianity is so meagre and confused, that it is difficult to understand how even the most illiterate and mystified sectary fed on apocryphal gospels could have conveyed to him such notions of the Gospel. Of the great enlightening history of Israel, as a history, he knows nothing and has merely caught up some childish tales from the Talmud and some garbled legends of the Hebrew patriarchs and great men " (pp 13-14).

In his own evaluation of the Quran, Thomas Carlyle (1795-1881), in his controversial work, *On Heroes and Hero Worship*, complains that the book is nothing but "a wearisome, long-winded entanglement; most crude and recondite; insupportable stupidity, in short."

Someone may ask: if this be so, why then do millions — even respectable and learned men — believe in the Quran as a holy book of God, and are ready to commit violence in order to defend it?

There are many reasons for this. Naturally, man prefers a religion that is in consonance with his wicked nature; a religion that appeals to the worst in him, approves of charms and violence, and yet makes him feel truly pious.

Moreover, there is an inherent power in repetition. When, for example, a lie — even an obvious lie, is repeated over and over again, it becomes convincing and believable. That is the psychology of advertising. The Russian psychologist, Pavlov, knew this, and his theory became the basis for the science of brainwashing used by the Communist world. It is a system being explored very well in Islam, and it works! The Muslim has been made to repeat certain things so much that it has become impossible for him to imagine the errancy of such statements. And believe me, he is ready to defend these 'truths' by any means. This power of repetition has been used to make even non-Muslims accept the claim that the Quran is elegant, really wonderful and non-pareil. But careful students have refused to be carried away by such cheap appraisals.

We have also discovered that there is nothing which is taught that would not get some followers, especially if it is consistent. That is why every philosopher, every cultist, will always have would be disciples, no matter how strict his terms may be.

Above all there is the fact that all lies are spiritual. This is because Satan, the father of all lies, is a spirit. That is why it takes a spiritual warfare to fight a lie. In the words of Thackeray: "A lie once set going, having the breath of life breathed into it by the father of lying, and ordered to run its diabolical little course, lives with a prodigious vitality."

Yes, a lie may continue to live. But any of the deceived victims has the will-power to get himself out of it! And if this book succeeds in getting the reader out of a popular deception, it has achieved its sole purpose.

"A lie should be trampled upon and extinguished wherever found. I am for fumigating the atmosphere, where I suspect falsehood, like pestilence, breathes around me." ——Carlyle.

CHAPTER TEN
What Difference Does It Make?

"And ye shall know the truth, and the truth shall make you free." (John 8:32).

UNLESS one wants to play syncretism,[1] which is a subterfuge, every serious thinker will agree that truth is bigoted by nature. It is intolerant in its relationship with a lie. It becomes particularly hard to swallow if heavy doses of a lie have been taken for too long a time.

Now, if one says the Islamic Allah is not the Christian God, what then is one saying? What now happens to the Arabic Bible, and the Hausa and Fulani Bibles which have the name 'ALLAH' running through their pages? Should they ignore that name and find a different name for the Holy God of Heaven and Earth?

Such a change may not be very simple, given how much and how long they have believed in this 'God'. One is surprised at how the Hausa language, for example, could be so Islamized. In Northern Nigeria, nearly every sentence in Hausa is punctuated with 'Allah'. Not many people even know that 'Allah' is not an Hausa word. A Christian sister even told us at a fellowship some-time ago that 'Allah' is the Hausa word for the Almighty God! We know that is not true. We are sure Hausa had a name for God before Islam came.

In the following two chapters, we shall try to examine the relationship between a word and its

---

1 Syncretism is the belief that there is truth in all religions: that everybody is worshipping God in his own way; and that all religions ultimately lead to the same God. No matter how popular this 'faith' is becoming today, and no matter who believes it, it is a doctrine of demons (John 14:6).

referent. For example, when a Muslim says 'Allah' who is he referring to (knowingly or ignorantly)? When an Hausa or Arab Christian says 'Allah', who is he referring to? Is it the same Allah of the Muslims?

In one of the theories of meaning in an aspect of linguistics known as semantics (or meanings of meaning), a word means its referent, that is the object it refers to — the object or image the word brings into our imagination. The linguistic strength of that theory is not our business here. But using this theory of meaning, we may ask: Who is the object of worship in Islam?

In all fairness, we have no doubt that most Muslims who say 'Allah' have in their mind the Creator of heaven and the earth. But is that sufficient to demonstrate that they are worshipping the same God as the Christians? What if the name 'SATAN' is used by some ignorant people to refer to the Creator-God, would that have made any difference? And what if someone believes in a wrong thing but is very sincere and honest about it, does it matter?

We believe that one hundred percent sincerity in what one believes does not make it right. One can indeed be sincerely wrong! We know every culture and people has the concept of a creator called by different names. But the problem most of them have is in their particular conception of such a creator. Some even have more than one creator. They think of that creator as the chief idol, and so carve some things to represent him. They make their supposed creator even uglier than they themselves, and they have to feed him with palm oil, goat meat and its blood, hens, etc.

But the God of the Bible says: *"I will take no bullock out of thy house, nor he goats out of thy folds. For every beast of the forest is mine, and the cattle upon a thousand hills. I know all the fowls of the mountains:*

and the wild beasts of the field are mine. If I were hungry, I would not tell thee: for the world is mine, and the fulness thereof. Will I eat the flesh of bulls, or drink the blood of goats?" (Psalm 50:9-13).

According to the Scripture, such people who ignore the Bible and 'make' God or gods are under the judgment of God, whatever culture they belong to, and whatever cosmology they hold on to: *"Because that which may be known of God is manifest in them; for God hath shewed it unto them. For the invisible things of him from the creation of the world are clearly seen, being understood by the things that are made, even his eternal power and Godhead; so that they are without excuse: Because that, when they knew God, they glorified Him not as God, neither were thankful; but became vain in their imagination, and their foolish heart was darkened. Professing themselves to be wise, they became fools, And changed the glory of the uncorruptible God into an image made like to corruptible man, and to birds, and four-footed beasts, and creeping things."* (Romans 1:19-23).

Some Christians even think that there is nothing behind idols; we know that is not true. An idol is nothing in itself but wood, clay, iron, bronze, etc. But whenever people make an idol and gather to worship it, Satan assigns demons who will be hovering around the shrine, influencing the lives of all those that come to worship there. These demons often possess the priests or priestesses and sometimes speak through them to the adherents, some demanding sacrifices or foretelling their future (1 Corinthians 10:19-21). All those dedicated to such gods are influenced for life by the spirits behind the idols, unless they are converted, prayed for specifically and set free.

Bible-believing Christians have often been accused of being narrow in their views about the true religion. In a way, our accusers are right because the way to heaven is indeed 'narrow' and 'strait' (Matt 7:14). The fact is that we need no further expansion of views beyond the words of our Lord, because the Holy Spirit witnesses to us that we have eternal life and so our views remain narrow.

In his attempt to look for support and dismiss the Christian view about other religions, our friend, Ahmed Deedat, quoting one of his heroes, says, "There never was a false god nor was there ever a false religion, unless you call a child a false man."[2]

Except at the surface level, this line of reasoning is false. We can gently disarm the argument by going to the Quran itself. In Surah 3:19, for example, we read, "True religion before God is Islam." That means that there can be a true religion. And if there can be a true religion, then there must be some false religions.

What then is a false religion? Since God is holy and man is sinful, we define a false religion as a religion that has not settled the sin question; a religion that has not taken lying, idolatry, pride, adultery, anger and all forms of wickedness from a man and yet promises that same man some euphoria here or in heaven. That is what should be considered a false religion.

In his Appendix and Commentary on the pre-Islamic Arabian gods in Surah 71:23, Yusuf Ali calls these gods "false gods" So, contrary to Deedat and his philosopher, Yusuf Ali says there can indeed be false gods.

Other evidence from the Quran which dismisses Ahmed Deedat's argument is seen in Surah 16:36, which says, "serve Allah and shun false gods" (M.M. Pickthall's translation) Drs Muhammad Al-Hilali & M. Muhsin Khan's translation renders it as "false deities".

2 Deedat, A. 'What is His Name?' p.3

Of course, there can be a false god, and even a false man! Every reality can have a false impression. Anything that looks real but is not, is false or fake. No one has ever seen God, for example. Therefore any physical image 'representing' him is false. Even when demons appear to people, they change their real features. A demon can be seen in different forms when appearing at different times. Any graphic picture of the devil is false because he changes physical form.

Who then is a worshipper of a false god? He is the one who worships an idol. If an idol is a false representation of God or a god, and the worshipper has never seen such a being in reality, it means that an idol is a false god. A doll, no matter how fine, is a false child, and a mannequin a false man.

Apart from physical images, if a man conceives of God as different from the one only true God of the Bible and worships such a 'God', no matter how sincere he may be, he is just like the one who has made a physical image to represent God. Any 'God' that emerges out of such imagination is a false god. Our knowledge of God is from revelation and not from imagination. A.W. Tozer says, "Do not try to imagine God or you will have an imaginary God."

God has revealed Himself in His Word, and in the Person of Jesus Christ. See Him there; know Him there. Since there is only one God, any physical image or any imagination or image of the mind that is different from this one real God is a false god. We maintain therefore that whether a man is imagining a god or carving a physical image of a god, he is making an image. A physical idol is, in fact, made like the idol in the mind of the artist. So, as a physical image can be a false god, so can a mental image be a false god.

In the Old Testament, Gideon destroyed images of a false god in Israel as we noted in Chapter Two of this book. In the New Testament, God does not command that the Christian should go from house to house destroying people's physical idols. Why? Because it is a useless exercise if the images still exist in the minds of the people.

And so the Bible talks of *"casting down imaginations"*, i.e. destroying false ideas about God in people's minds, and presenting to them the correct idea about the Creator and the creation. This is the primary duty of the Christian, and the particular duty of this writer. God has called us to be involved in this end-time mass iconoclasm, casting down false gods and false paradises in people's minds. In the words of Jock Anderson, we insist that, "If there is a God at all, then we need not a caricature of him, but a true representation, and some means of recognising him"[3]

The Name Of The Lord

God told Moses His name was *"I AM THAT I AM"*, the name He said He did not reveal to Abraham and other people who had served Him. Tell them "I AM hath sent me unto you." (Exodus 3:14). That probably sounds strange. Actually, God may not need a personal name since there are no other Gods. All the so-called Gods of the heathen are idols and they are nothing more than demonic spirits whose judgment has long been settled (1 Corinthians 10:19-20; Matthew 8:29).

This is one of the areas where the 'Jehovah's Witnesses' are wrong. They will never use any name for God other than JEHOVAH. We know it was the

3 Anderson, Jock *'Worship the Lord'*, Inter-Varsity Press, London p.25

ancient Hebrew translators of the Old Testament (The Masoretes) that used the name JEHOVAH. The King James Version translators used 'the LORD' or 'GOD' (written in small capitals). It is said that the name JEHOVAH was originally pronounced YAHWEH or JAHWEH which was written without the vowels for fear of pronouncing it wrongly, thus 'misusing the name of the LORD' as in the Third Commandment. In its place, the Hebrew word Elohim was used, especially when speaking.

God surely reveals Himself by name, but more importantly, by His divine nature and His Word and the Law. If there are many names for God, such names MUST refer to the God of the Bible or they are not God's names at all. The God of heaven has been called by different names in different languages. But that has not hindered the relationship too significantly or their understanding of Him, since God has deliberately split the human language into many different tongues. He may not expect us all to use the same name for Him all over the world.

But it is still significant to note that in the Ogu language (erroneously but popularly called Egun, spoken in Badagry in Nigeria and the Republic of Benin), the name of God is JEWHE or YEWEH and MAWU. We note that the first two names sound like the Hebrew YAHWEH and JAHWEH. It is an established fact in linguistics that J=Y=I, and W=V=U in certain language groups. And they already had these names in the Ogu language before the Europeans could think of coming to Africa with the Bible! Even when they came, they did not introduce the Hebrew name for God, but simply 'God' and His 'Jesus'. Surely, therefore, God reveals Himself to all those who diligently seek him in simplicity of faith (Hebrews 11:6).

Historians, like Vaqqidi, have said that Allah was actually the chief of the 360 gods being worshipped in Arabia at the time Mohammed rose to prominence. Ibn Al-Kalbi gave 27 names of pre-Islamic deities. From the Quran itself, we can name up to nine of these idols. The Ka'ba, housing many of these gods, has remained the temple of Allah which Muslims revere and go to worship and kiss in Mecca during the Hajj. It is significant that even if a Muslim is not in Mecca, he has to face the direction of the shrine, the Ka'ba, while praying, every time. History records that pagans in Arabia had been visiting the Ka'ba on pilgrimage before Islam started. Mecca was a commercial centre at the time, and foreign merchants and Arabians faced the Ka'ba in prayer because that was where most of their gods were deposited. Many of the gods were brought by these merchants from their countries.

Interestingly, not many Muslims want to accept that Allah was already being worshipped at the Ka'ba in Mecca by Arab pagans before Mohammed came. Some Muslims become angry when they are confronted with this fact. But history is not on their side. Pre-Islamic literature has proved this. In the Quran itself, we see that pre-Islamic Arabs made their strongest oaths in the name of Allah because they believed he was the most powerful of their gods (Surah 6:109). He was already regarded by the pagans as the creator, the lord of the shrine, Ka'ba, and the city of Mecca. Ka'ba was known as 'baithu'llah' ('house of allah'). All other idol shrines in other regions in Arabia were also called "baithullah" (Surah 106:3; 27:91; 6:109). Apart from Allah, other major deities worshipped at Mecca are Al-lat or Allat, the feminine form of the Arabic word 'allah', al-Uzza and al-Manat, three female idols being worshipped inside the Ka'ba.

According to al-Tabari, the gharaniq (female) idols were even regarded as daughters of Allah. Other popular idols were Wadd, Suwa, Yaguth, Ya'uq, Nasr and Hubal, to which Mohammed's wife, Khadijah, also sacrificed and worshipped because her sons were dying young (Surah 71:23; Haykal, Mohammed. *The Life of Muhammad,* P. 69).

One other proof that Allah was already being worshipped as an idol in Arabia is in the fact that Mohammed's father was called Abdallah or Abdullah meaning 'the servant or slave of Allah'.

Some have taken this to mean that Allah must therefore be the Almighty God. But this only shows that Allah was already known in Arabia to be a supernatural being. It is NOT a proof that he is God Almighty.

Ibn Ishaq is the earliest biographer of Mohammed and his work *Surahtu'l Rasul* (A.D. 768), which we have already referred to, is one of the most authentic records of the history of Mohammed. In this work,[4] we read that Abdul Muttalib, Mohammed's paternal grandfather, had vowed to sacrifice a son to Allah if he was protected from his people who were opposing his Zamzam well project. When he eventually succeeded in the work and also had the sons, he brought them into the Ka'ba and "stood by Hubal praying to Allah" while lots were being cast to determine which son would be sacrificed. The image of Hubal was there. The lot fell on Abdullah. He was then taken before two other idols, Isaf and Na'ila for slaughtering. Some people protested, and further leading had to be obtained to establish what to do. Abdullah was then taken to "the Hijaz, for there there was a sorceress who had a familiar

---

4 Guillaume, A. *The Life of Muhammad,* a translation of Ibn Ishaq's, Oxford University Press 1955) pp.66-68

spirit". The woman needed some time to consult her familiar spirit (a demon) to know what Allah would say as to whether or not the child must still be slaughtered for him. "When they had left her, Abdul Muttalib prayed to Allah, and when they visited her the next day, she said, 'Word has come to me...'". She said several camels should be sacrificed "until your lord is satisfied". This was done and Abdullah was spared. But from that time, he was dedicated to "the lord". He grew up and brought forth Mohammed.

In this revealing incident in the life of Mohammed's grandfather, who was "the lord"? Was it Allah? What about Hubal?

It has been suggested by Pockock that the word 'Hubal' could be from Ha-Baal or HuBaal in Hebrew (meaning 'the lord'), a Moabite god that was imported into many nations, including Israel. God destroyed the Israelites for involving themselves in the worship of this god (Numbers 25:1-3). From Ibn Ishaq's account here, praying to Allah was the same thing as praying to Hubal. They could practically mean the same thing. As Ha-Baal or Hu-Baal means 'the lord', so "al-ilah" or "al'lah" means 'the god'.

It is interesting that many Muslim leaders are afraid of carrying out any thorough research into the origin of Islam, especially, the pre-Islamic Arabian religion, in case they discover anything that will cause their faith in Islam to wane. Since they have refused to do such research, Western scholars have been doing it for them.

We wish that Muslim readers would consider the following questions seriously. Why does Islam regard the Moon as sacred? Why are many Muslim priests astrologers? What link has the Islamic religion and Allah with the Crescent Moon and Star symbols as seen on the minarets and domes of their mosques everywhere, and also on the flags of Islamic nations? What link is there between the Moon and the Rhamadan fast?

Professor A. Guilluame, an expert in the studies of the Islamic religion, says the worship of the moon god was rampant in Arabia at the time of Mohammed. According to him, the moon god had several names, one of which was 'Allah'.

Also, Middle East scholar, E.M. Wherry, in his monumental work, *A Comprehensive Commentary on the Quran* shows that the worship of Allah and the worship of Ba-al (Huba'l) involved the worship of the heavenly bodies the moon, the stars and the sun.

So, on the issue of Muttalib's son, Mohammed's father bearing the name 'Abdallah', it may simply be like some people in Nigeria bearing the names Sangoloni, Esubiyi, Orogbemi, Ifagbamila, Ogungbe, Odugbemi, etc., meaning: Sango-owns-this, Begotten-of-Satan, Oro-honours-me, Ifa-has-saved me, etc. All these are Yoruba names given to children from a specific idolatrous family, and they have no connection with God Almighty, but to specific idols that people revere as their gods whom they are serving.

Therefore, we submit that the fact that someone was called Abdallah is NOT a proof that 'Allah' is the Almighty God of the Bible. It only proves that 'Allah' was already known as a supernatural being before Islam started; and a supernatural being can be any spirit. Since Abdallah was in the service of the Ka'ba shrine, the Allah he was serving must have been one of the gods of the shrine! This is a much more probable and logical view. The father was 'Abd ul allah', servant of Allah, the son was 'rasul 'llah', apostle of Allah.

God told Moses: *"I am the God of thy father"* (Exodus 3:6). Allah also revealed himself to Mohammed as the god of his father Abdallah. The question is: who is this god, the Allah that Mohammed's father was worshipping and serving?

It is true that Meccans wanted to kill Mohammed. But these Meccans were not against the worship of Allah. They were already worshipping him. All they resisted was what they felt to be the new undue monopoly Mohammed was seemingly imposing on Allah to enjoy over other gods in the shrine. That was why they threatened the life of the new prophet. And since Mohammed grew to know that his father was a servant of Allah, it is only logical that Allah should be the only god that must be worshipped. There should be no other god except Allah, and Mohammed should be the Prophet (*La illaha il allah, Muhammad rasul 'llah*). By becoming a prophet or servant of Allah, Mohammed was probably revolutionarily succeeding his father, whom he did not grow up to know.

God appeared to Abram and asked him to leave his relatives in the idolatrous town of Ur and go to a land He was to show him. God was careful not to say He was the god of Abram's father. This was because Abram's father, Terah, was an idolater.

If Abram had lived in Mecca, would God have appeared to him as Allah? That is the 'theological question'. Abram left idolatry and began to live and worship God in faith. He is known as the father of faith, and so could not have worshipped a stone as Muslims allege. Probably in an attempt to justify the worship of the Moon, the Quran presents Abraham as addressing the moon and the sun as "my Lord". Jews and Christians know Abraham never worshipped or venerated the moon; and he never worshipped the Black Stone in Mecca.

We wish to ask our Muslim friends: Why do you go all the way to Saudi Arabia to dance and chant round a stone if you have some big ones in your own country?

The African Muslim is told that the stones in his village are idols and should not be worshipped or offered sacrifice; but that the stone in another country, Saudi Arabia, is not an idol when worshipped, kissed and offered sacrifice. Every year, hundreds of thousands flood Mecca, paying huge sums of money to airlines and into the Saudi treasury for the Hajj. Many Muslims are really zealous and sincere, and some have to borrow the money for the Hajj, enduring all the hazards of the Pilgrimage. They have been deceived: their own local stones are idols; but the one in Saudi is not. That is the message, and it is simple.

When God was sending Moses to the Israelites in Egypt, He told Moses to introduce Him to the Israelites as the God of their forefathers. But God was very careful to cite specifically the forefathers He was referring to. He said that He was, and is, the God of Abraham, Isaac and Jacob (Exodus 3:6).

Egyptians, no doubt, had a name for the supposed Creator of heaven and earth, and the Israelites must have been acquainted with this name. Moses himself had lived in Egypt for forty years and knew everything about the religion and gods of the land. But Moses did not go to these people and claim that one of the common great gods of Egypt had revealed himself to him. He introduced another name entirely. When he approached Pharaoh, he did not go in the name of the chief god of Egypt. He went with the name of a different God he had encountered: *"And afterward Moses and Aaron went in, and told Pharaoh, Thus saith the LORD God of Israel, Let my people go, that they may hold a feast unto me in the wilderness. And Pharaoh said, Who is the LORD, that I should obey his voice to let Israel go? I know not the LORD, neither will I let Israel go."* (Exodus 5:1-2). Pharaoh would not have dared ask such a question if Moses had appeared in the name of any of the gods of Egypt.

We would be wrong therefore to imagine that there is nothing in a name.

Mohammed rose up to proclaim a message from Allah, the god of the Ka'ba shrine that his father had been dedicated to. He insisted that only Allah should be worshipped. By his military prowess, he succeeded in bringing the Meccans into submission. But even though all the images in the Ka'ba shrine were removed during his second pilgrimage from Medina to Mecca, yet all the idolatrous rituals in the shrine during pre-Islamic pilgrimages remain the same even today. In a discussion, a former Muslim woman who is now a Christian told me personally that when she went to Mecca for the Hajj, she refused to perform the rituals at the Ka'ba because she felt a strong aura of traditional idolatry that she had been involved in before. She stayed most of the time in her hostel. She had been told in Islam that Christians are idolaters because they accord to Jesus the same worship they give to God. But with her own experience of the rituals during the Hajj, the whole institution of her religion seemed to be an organised 'monotheistic idolatry' on an international scale. Her people seemed to her more guilty of idolatry than the Christians that they accused of the same. From there, she had to find out more about the Christian faith, and eventually was converted.

We have wondered why committed Muslims never like substituting any other name for the name of Allah. Therefore, next, we examine further whether a particular name really matters in worship.

CHAPTER ELEVEN

What Is In A Name?

SOMEONE may ask why we have to bother ourselves with a name. What is in a name? I believe there
is a lot in a name. The Bible says, *"The name of the
LORD is a strong tower; the righteous runneth into it and
is safe."* (Proverbs 18:10). But how can one run into it
and be safe if one does not know the name?

Jesus asked Christians to baptise new believers
*"in the name of the Father, and of the Son, and of the
Holy Ghost."* (Matthew 28:19). Again, the Scripture
says, *"for there is none other name under heaven given
among men, whereby we must be saved."* (Acts 4:12).
Jesus says: *"In my name, they* (believers in Him)
shall cast out devils." (Mark 16:17). Can the name of
Allah be used to cast out demons?

It is also written: *"At the name of Jesus every knee
should bow."* (Philippians 2:10).

Does the devil fear the name of Allah? If not, then
it is not the name of the LORD that Jesus came to
represent. Jesus said: *"After this manner therefore pray ye:
Our Father which art in heaven, Hallowed be thy Name."*
(Matthew 6:9). But He did not give us any Name!
Why? God's name as a Father is a new revelation,
and it is a revelation in the heart of a person who has
become His child. Perhaps the first test that the Allah
of Mohammed fails is that he is not a Father. If a
Muslim says, 'Our Father who is in heaven' his own
heart will rebel against it immediately. He can't
continue that prayer with his heart because he does
not possess the Name of the Father.

For those who contend that 'Allah' is simply the
Arabic translation of the name of the LORD, we
say it is not 'simply' so. 'Allah' is more than a
translation.

Pastor Richard Wurmbrand says God has many aliases. But is 'Allah' one of those aliases? Is the God of the Bible the being behind the Islamic Allah? Any translation of the name of God must carry the same authority as the original Name.

Why 'Isa?

Careful linguists have wondered, rightly, why the Quran has to refer to Jesus as 'Isa. Following the linguistic principles of the Semitic languages such as Hebrew, Assyrian, Aramaic, Arabic, Ethiopian, Phoenician, 'Isa is not the Arabic translation of Jesus, Jesu, or the Greek Iesous. It is Yesou or Yesu', as has been rightly used by the Arabic translators of the New Testament.

Mohammed was probably confused with the name "Esau" that the unbelieving Jews in Yathrib were using disparagingly to refer to Jesus. Since the Jews rejected Jesus as their Lord and Master, they regarded Him as a type of Esau, the rejected brother of Jacob (Israel). 'Isa or Ai'sa or Essa were translations of the "Esau", the 'Jesus' that the Jews talked about as the founder of Christianity. Such an obvious mis- take makes one again question the divine origin of the Quran.

The Power In A Name

The psalmist declared in adoration: *"O LORD our Lord, how excellent is thy name in all the earth!"* (Psalm 8:1). The Hebrew equivalents of the name of JESUS are Joshua, Jeshua or Jeho-shua or Jehovah-shua — meaning, Jehovah-saves, or 'Jehovah-delivers' (Matthew 1:21). The Greek is *Iesous ho Christos.* The English version, Jesus, the Christ; the Yoruba version Jesu Kristi; the Ogu (Egun) version, Jesu Klisti;[1] the Hausa translation,

---
1 Egun has no 'r' sound

Yesu; and all other versions referring to the same Lord, carry the same weight and perform the same functions — saving and delivering from sin, sickness, Satan and evil spirits.

We should realise that there were other people with the name 'Jesus' during the time of our Lord. But when 'Jesus Christ', or literally, 'Jesus, the Christ', is mentioned or even 'Jesus' alone is mentioned by a Christian, and it is referring to the Lord, it will perform the same functions. As a believer in Jesus Christ no demon can question me about which 'Jesus' I mean if I cast it out in that name. Even when the sons of Sceva of Acts 19 asked some demons to come out of a mad man, the demons didn't ask them which Jesus. The men were disgraced only because they were not Christians and had no Spirit of Christ inside them to cast out evil spirits.

Moses did not have the name JESUS. No other prophet used that name. The name God gave Moses, as we noted earlier, was *"I AM THAT I AM"*, and Moses used that name to deliver a whole nation and to disgrace the magicians and occultists of the heathen land, Egypt. Young David told giant Goliath, *'I come to you in THE NAME OF THE LORD', and he delivered a nation* (1 Samuel 17:45).

If the name of Allah cannot save or deliver, what then can it do? According to those who had gone deep into Islam before their conversion, the name of Allah is used by Muslim occultists to make incantations and charms. The name of our own Saviour is used for good things.

Peter told the government officials and religious people who arrested him and John: *"Be it known unto you all, and to all the people of Israel, that by the name of Jesus Christ of Nazareth, whom ye crucified, whom God raised from the dead, even by him doth this*

(formerly crippled) *man stand here before you whole …
Now when they saw the boldness of Peter and John, and
perceived that they were unlearned and ignorant men,
they marvelled; and they took knowledge of them, that
they had been with Jesus. And beholding the man which
was healed standing with them, they could say nothing
against it. But when they had commanded them to go
aside out of the council, they conferred among
themselves. Saying, What shall we do to these men? for
that indeed a notable miracle hath been done by them is
manifest to all them that dwell in Jerusalem: and we
cannot deny it. But that it spread no further among the
people, let us straitly threaten them, that they speak
henceforth to no man in this name."* (Acts 4:10, 13-17).

Just like these godless religious people threatening
the early Christians, it seems there is something in
Muslims that hates the name JESUS. Even if you gave
a Muslim beggar some money and you mention the
name of Jesus with it, he would reject it. If he is
particularly hungry, he may collect it, but he would
wash the money before spending it.

Is The Word Allah In The 'original' Bible?

The vociferous South African Muslim Jihâdist, Ahmed
Deedat, wrote a whole pamphlet[2] to ridicule the
Christian God and to show his readers that the Arabic
'Allah' is right there in the 'corrupted' Christian Bible.

As if he is coming to give the shocker of the century,
Deedat announces on page three of his pamphlet: "It

---

2 Deedat, A. *'What is His Name?'* — This and many other
books like *The God That Never Was* by Ahmed Deedat,are
deliberately written to mock the Christian concept of God,
and to particularly ridicule the Deity of our Lord Jesus
Christ. Yet Deedat and many Muslim writers of his like do
not realise that their Quran warns, "Revile not ye those
whom they call upon besides God, lest they out of spite
revile God in their ignorance."(Surah 6:108).

is enough, for the moment, to say that in the language of Moses, Jesus and Mohammed...the name of God Almighty is ALLAH."

What is that 'shocker'? It is the presence of the Hebrew words elohim, elah, and alah in a footnote in an earlier edition of the Schofield Commentary Bible. Deedat concludes from the footnote that these words mean the Arabic 'Allah'. I have seen this particular point repeated in at least two of his publications.

Deedat has tried to convince his readers that he is a wonderful scholar of comparative religion. It seems, however, that much of his argument falls to the ground. The words are in the footnotes and not part of the text of the Bible. And according to the editors of the same edition of the Schofield Bible, while the first two words mean 'God', 'alah', on the other hand, is a common Hebrew word meaning 'to swear'. Moreover, it is a verb and not a noun as Deedat thinks. And the editors do not suggest that those three words mean 'Allah'.

Deedat knows his readers and pupils do not know Biblical Hebrew, and he is smart at riding on their intelligence. This is the same method that the Jehovah Witnesses use to spread their wrong doctrines.

First, the word 'elah' in Hebrew means an oak or terebinth, and it is a close morpheme. That is, it is a complete grammatical unit in itself. The only sense in which an oak can be associated with an attribute of God is its representation of strength.

The word is also used for the personal names of some particular individuals in the Bible. For example, in Genesis 36:41, 'Elah' is given as one of the dukes of Edom. In 1 Samuel 17:2,19, we have "the valley of Elah". In 1 Chronicles 4:15, we have the son of Caleb bearing Elah. In 1 Chronicles 9:8, a Benjamite is also called Elah. The father of Shimei is called Elah (1 Kings 4:18); one of the kings of Israel is also called Elah. The father of Hoshea in 2 Kings 15:30 is also Elah.

Jesus said, *"Hallowed be Thy Name"*. If the Lord's Name must be hallowed, we do not expect that Name to be given indiscriminately to human beings. Neither could it be the name of a tree which anybody could mention any time. God had commanded Israel not to take the name of the Lord their God in vain; and if we realise that Jews were afraid to even mention the covenant Name of the Lord, then we should know it would be impossible for them to give this same name or a similar one to their children.

In reference to God, the word 'elah' is introduced in Ezra 4:24 and used 43 times in that book alone. Another place where this word occurs is in Daniel where it appears 45 times. One significant point to note here is that these two books were written by people who had been in a foreign land (Babylon or Persia) for 70 years. Although they still believed strongly in their God, their language had been greatly influenced. The last place this word appears is in Jeremiah 10:11. Jeremiah's use of the word is significant. Here the prophet used it in the plural to refer to false gods: *"Thus shall ye say unto them, The gods that have not made the heavens and the earth, even they shall perish from the earth, and from under these heavens."* A similar word, Eloah, is used 56 times in the Old Testament. It was first used in Deuteronomy 32:15 and appears 41 times in the book of Job.

All the other times the word 'elah' is used in the original Hebrew texts, it refers directly to the oak tree. In Amos 2:9, God reminds the children of Israel of the conquests He had wrought for them:

"Yet destroyed I the Amorite before them, whose height was like the height of the cedars, and he was strong as the oaks (Hebrew plural: elahim); *yet I destroyed his fruit from above, and his roots from beneath."*

If 'elah' were the name of God, He would not have said He destroyed the Amorites as elah.

In Isaiah 1:29, God said: *"For they shall be ashamed of the oaks* (Hebrew: elah); *which ye have desired, and ye shall be confounded for the gardens that ye have chosen."*

God's name is honourable, majestic and excellent in all the earth (Psalm 8:1); and if elah were His Name or even one of His names, he could not have used it as seen above.

It is also very significant to note that elah is actually used in Isaiah 44:14 as referring to a place of idolatry where man had hewn down many 'elahim' to make a religion out of them. God actually derides man for making a god out of elah:

"Then shall it be for a man to burn: for he will take thereof, and warm himself; yea, he kindleth it, and baketh bread; yea, he maketh a god, and worshippeth it; he maketh it a graven image, and falleth down thereto. He burneth part thereof in the fire; with part thereof he eateth flesh; he roasteth roast, and is satisfied: yea, he warmeth himself, and saith, Aha, I am warm, I have seen the fire: And the residue thereof he maketh a god, even his graven image: he falleth down unto it, and worshippeth it, and prayeth unto it, and saith, Deliver me; for thou art my god. They have not known nor understood: for he hath shut their eyes, that they cannot see; and their hearts, that they cannot understand. And none considereth in his heart, neither is there knowledge nor understanding to say, I have burned part of it in the fire; yea, also I have baked bread upon the coals thereof; I have roasted flesh, and eaten it: and shall I make the residue thereof an abomination? shall I fall down to the stock of a tree?" (Isaiah 44:15-19).

If the elah of the Bible is the Allah of Muslims; if he is the god of the Black Stone in Mecca, the baithullah of the Ka'ba shrine which pagans were worshipping in Arabia and which Muslims worship, he surely is not the 'El' and the 'Jah' of the Bible. In Hebrew, it is 'El' that was used to refer to God, and it is never used in isolation to refer to any other person, place or thing. It is usually used as an affix when used to refer to a person. For example, there is Elkana — God has possessed (used in eight places), Elnathan — God has given, Eltolad — kindred of God, etc.

The nearest word to 'El' given to a human being is 'Eli', and it means 'God is high', or when written differently, it means 'my God'. Some like Deedat may claim that 'Eli' sounds like 'Allah', but the 'i' included (written and called Yodh) is not part of the word and it is usually a predicator or a modal as in 'Elijah' ('El is Jah', or 'God is the LORD').

We stress again that the 'i' in 'Eli' is not part of the word, but a suffix. When Jesus cried "Eli" or "Eloi" on the cross, he was not saying "God, God", but "My God, my God". This is another area where Deedat misses the point in his pamphlet. The Hebrew word used for God in Genesis 1:1 is 'Elohim' — not 'Allah', 'allah' or 'elah' and appears 32 times in Genesis chapter one alone. Altogether it appears 2,570 times in the Old Testament. IT IS A PLURAL WORD WHICH ESTABLISHES THE PLURALITY IN UNITY OF DEITY. This negates any identity with the Allah of the Quran because, grammatically, the word 'Allah' does not even allow plurality.

The linguistic analysis of the Arabic 'Allah' will probably take a separate Ph.D thesis in itself. But, briefly, let us take the study from the very popular faith confession of Islam: 'La ilaha illa allah...'

148

La = no

ilaha = probably from ilahun, meaning 'a god'

illa or il' = except or but;

Then the crucial word "allah". Most scholars agree that it is a combination of two words 'al' which is the Arabic for the definite article (determinant) 'the', and 'ilaha', "god", making 'al-ilaha' or al'laha or al-illah, i.e. 'the god'. This possibly became 'allah'. The correct translation of the *Confession* will therefore be 'there is no god except the god'.

This explanation holds good if, and only if, the word 'allah' is truly of Arabic origin. Some linguists, however, believe that the word does not have an Arabic origin, but is taken from one of the Semitic languages.[3] The closest linguistic probability is that the name might have been a variant of the Syriac word, 'alaha', which was used to refer to God, and was already in use by Christians before Islam came. But even this is only a linguistic probability, and may have nothing to do with the referent of the Islamic 'Allah' - the Christ-denying Allah of Mohammed, the Allah that denies that Jesus came as God in the flesh. In fact, many scholars have dissociated the Syriac word from the Arabian Allah.

"Yah Allahu"

We are surprised at how far Ahmed Deedat could go in wrenching words to prove his bold assertions. Take for example, the expression 'Halleluyah' as he explains in his pamphlet *What is His Name?* He says the 'yah' simply means 'oh' or an exclamatory particle (!). He says the Apostle John sounds

3 Jeffery, A. *'Foreign Vocabulary of the Qur'an'* Al-Biruni, Lahore (1977)

ridiculous by claiming in Revelation chapter 19 that the angels and the saints in Heaven are shouting Halleluyah, which he claims is simply equivalent to the English 'hip, hip, hurray!' How could angels of God be shouting 'hip, hip, hurray!' to worship God? he queries. The same pamphlet also goes on to say that the expression 'Halleluyah' is a corruption of what he coins as 'Ya Allahu' which he says means 'Oh Allah!' All these claims are a vestige of ignorance. First, John wrote the book of Revelation in Greek and not in Hebrew, and the word he used is 'alleluia'. It is the Greek form of the Hebrew 'Hallelujah' or 'Halleluyah'. Moreover, it was not John that introduced the expression.

The Hebrew texts of the Old Testament written several hundreds of years before John was born are full of this expression, especially the Psalms. It is an expression of praise to God, and contrary to Deedat's claims, it is meaningful! It is not simply 'hip, hip, hurray' as Deedat claims. The Hebrew manuscripts have it as 'Hallelu Yah'. Actually, there are three words there. The lexical words are 'hallel' and 'yah'. 'Hallel' (pronounced /haleil/), means 'praise' in Hebrew. Psalm 136, for example, is sometimes called "the Hallel" because it is an antiphonal psalm of praise. Psalms 120-136 are sometimes jointly called the "Great Hallel" because they are peculiarly psalms of praise. The second lexical item, 'Yah' is the short form of 'Yahweh' and a variation of 'Jah', meaning 'the LORD'. It is from these we have 'Hallel u Yah', 'praise ye the LORD'.

In the Hebrew texts, 'Halleluyah' is found in the last line of Psalm 104. It is also used in the first and forty-eighth verses of Psalm 106, and the beginning of Psalms 111, 112, 113, the last line of Psalms 115, 116, and 117; verses 1,3 and 21 of Psalm 135; first and last lines of Psalms 146, 147, 148 and 150!

It sounds preposterous, therefore, to hear Ahmed Deedat saying 'Halleluyah' simply means 'Oh Allah.' In his debate with Dr Anis Shorrosh in London in 1985, Deedat said: "'Jah' is an expression in Arabic as 'Oh, mother'. Allelujah means 'Yah is Allah', there is no other God."[4] You wonder what he is actually saying? I think, however, that Mr Deedat is worth a good Islamic literary award for his aggressiveness and his ability to play deception and confuse even great minds. He deserves more oil money and a red feather on his turban.

'Allah' And Christian Worship

One must confess that this issue of the identity of Allah is very disturbing indeed. How can we be aware of the foregoing points and not develop an aversion towards the very name itself? And if we do, how do we communicate the Gospel to Hausas or Arabs without using the word? Moreover, there are still many languages that have not got a translation of the Bible, and we seem to bother our heads about the existing ones because of a name purported to be referring to God.

In Malaysia since 1981 the Bible or 'Al-Kitab' has been banned in the Malay language. The reason: Because it has in it the word "Allah" as well as some other words that have Islamic origin. There is now a law in that country in which Islam claims 50% of the population, that henceforth, no religion other than Islam may use certain words including 'Allah', 'faith' and 'belief' in its literature. Obviously, this law was inspired by Satan in order to prevent the communication of the Gospel to Muslims. The question then becomes: Is it impossible to preach to

4 Shorrosh, A. *'Islam Revealed'* Thomas Nelson, Nashville, (1989) p.267

people who believe the Creator to be Allah without the use of that name? Should we expunge the name from our Bibles and find some other descriptive names for God?

In the Christian world itself, should we continue to use the name of Allah in our Church services? Or do we have to reduce the Godhead to the limitation of human language? What now happens to Hausa Christians or Christian Arabs who have grown up to recognise the Supreme Being as Allah? What if they continue to believe sincerely in Allah as the God and Father of our Lord Jesus and worship him in Spirit and in truth? Would there be any problem? These are not simple questions. Some have even wondered whether in fact one can worship God in Spirit and in truth in the name of Allah.

Jesus has said: *"For where two or three are gathered together in my name, there am I in the midst of them."* (Matt 18:20). What if we gather in the names of both the Lord Jesus and Allah? Whatever the case may be, I think there must be an inseparability between the name we use for God and the name of Jesus. In John 17:11, the Lord prays: *"..Holy Father, keep through thine own name those whom thou hast given me, that they may be one, as we are."*

At present, we need not impose an opinion on the use of 'Allah' in our worship. Yet we need to realise that the name matters in worship and adoration. Even idol worshippers know this. Can we use the name Eck, the 'god' in Eckankar, in our services and pretend it doesn't matter? What prevents us from using Krishna, Shiva, Vishnu, Devi, Brahman — the Hindus' so called manifestations of 'the one god'? Those who think that these names can be used in Christian worship have fallen into the snare of the Antichrist's interfaith theology now sweeping the European world. As I was becoming disturbed by this issue, the Spirit of the Lord gave me three specific Scriptures.

First, Zechariah 14:9. Here, Zechariah prophesies that when Jesus comes back, *"the LORD shall be king over all the earth: in that day shall there be one LORD, and his name one."* Hallelujah!

In the second Scripture, Zephaniah 3:9, God says, *"For then will I turn to the people a pure language, that they may all call upon the name of the LORD to serve him with one consent."* From this Scripture, we should note that the only reason given for restoring a pure language is to have the correct Name of God in worship.

In the third Scripture, Isaiah 65:16, the Lord explains that the other reason why He would do something about our language is *"That he who blesseth himself in the earth shall bless himself in the God of truth; and he that sweareth in the earth shall swear by the God of truth;"*

In other words, there will be no more confusion or deception as to who Allah really is in Islam or in Christianity. There will simply be no more 'Allah'. Whatever the historical background of a people, nobody must mention that name again or the name of any other god different from the God of truth. Already, God has warned Israel He must not hear the mention of any other god in their mouths. (Exodus 23:13).

When Jesus comes, the name of Allah will simply no longer exist in any version of the Arabic, Indonesian or Hausa Bibles. All our holy choruses and hymns with the name of Allah will either be abandoned or recomposed. That will be the divine decree. We won't need to engage in any theological acrobatics or present any polemics to convince anybody. It will be enforced *"over all the earth"*. Amen. *"That at the name of Jesus, every knee should bow, of things in heaven, and things in earth, and things under the earth; And that every tongue should confess that Jesus Christ is Lord, to the glory of God the Father."* (Philippians 2:10-11).

The psalmist says, *"Their sorrows shall be multiplied that hasten after another god: Their drink offerings of blood will I not offer, nor take up their names into my lips,"* (Psalms 16:4).

CHAPTER TWELVE

The Visions Of Mohammed

"For all the gods of the nations are idols: but the LORD made the heavens." (Psalm 96:5).

IF one worships the chief idol of a land, what difference does it make? How is one different from the person who worships many idols or claims to worship no god at all?

In his book on world religions, veteran missionary evangelist Dr Lester Sumrall, commenting in this regard, says: "Muslims worship one god and we (Christians) worship one God, but there all similarity ends. Mohammed's 'god' is radically different from God as He is revealed to us by the Bible. Mohammed's god is a spiteful, selfish autocrat who must be placated with a monotonous routine of holy motions. The God we worship is a loving, compassionate Father who asks only that we love Him in return",[1] and obey Him. *"If ye love me, keep my commandments."* (John 14:15).

We thank God for this serious observation and comment. It has served to reinforce our convictions on the spirit behind Islam. But there is still a question whether indeed it is only one god that is worshipped in Islam. One fact we need to realise is that one cannot serve the devil and worship him ONLY. If the devil is worshipped in any guise, he is worshipped through devils. There is in reality no monotheism, or more appropriately: monolatry, in heathenism. One cannot serve Satan and not have a relationship with demons. In fact, most operations and interactions in the occult and all Christless religions are more with these demonic spirits than with Satan himself. This is because Satan is not

1 Sumrall, L. *'Where was God when Pagan Religions Began?'* p.141.

omnipresent. He is not God, but an angel, a fallen angel for that matter. He cannot be in all places at the same time.

We don't know why Muslims think there is anything so new and wonderful in their assertion of the oneness of God. Jews also believe there is only one God. As Muslims chant their creed, '*la illaha...*', so do the Jews in their synagogues chant, "*Huh echad veein sheni*," "He is one and there is no second". But that does not mean they were serving God when they rejected Jesus. Even in the obviously polytheistic Hindu religion we find similar confessions in the Vedas, their sacred books; and also Hinduism had been existing for centuries before Islam started. So what is the new thing Islam is proclaiming by its claim of "no other god but Allah"? Any religion can say that its god is the only one existing and there is no other. The Bible says the claim of a belief in one God is not sufficient to take a man to Heaven. Man must believe in the one real and true God.

"*Thou believest that there is one God; thou doest well: the devils also believe, and tremble.*" (James 2:19). If therefore Muslims worship a god other than the one and the only revealed God of the Bible, they are not monotheists at all, whether they realise it or not.

Who Is To Blame?

Now if Mohammed introduced a wrong god, whose fault could that be? Why did the true God not reveal Himself to him and the Arabs? Or did he? And if God did not, will He be just to condemn Muslims on the day of Judgment?

History records that Mohammed, after acquiring much wealth from his caravan trade, left his business in search of spiritual realities — as many people do today, getting themselves involved in psychic practices when they get disenchanted and fed up with material things. He belonged to the Hanifas, or 'seekers of truth', a group of agnostics of his time. It was the practice of this group of people to be seeking light through inner consciousness and meditation. Much of the Hindu religion had passed through the Middle East on its way toward Europe, and left behind the teachings of the techniques of detaching oneself from the world of things and ideas, or 'maya'. After leaving his business Mohammed spent most of his time meditating in the Cave of Hira, about three miles from the city of Mecca. It was during one of his meditations that he was said to have been called to preach.

Who was the being that called him? And what was he commanded to preach? It is what he preached that will help us further determine whose messages he was carrying, the same messages we have been examining in the preceding chapters. It is the type of meditation a person is involved in that will determine who can speak to him and which being(s) he may come into contact with.

What Meditators Say

Swedish former occultist and Meditation teacher, Valter Ohman, after his conversion to Christianity, said: "If meditation is not thoroughly Christian, it leads to pagan communion with spirits. Meditation based on a false ideology brings people into contact with false spirits and a false god. The result is not liberation but oppression and possession."

West Indian Hindu yogi, Guru Rabindranath R. Maharaj, after giving his life to Christ, wrote in his autobiography: "I now understood that these were beings I had met in yogic trance and deep meditation, masquerading as Shiva or some other Hindu deity."

The renowned Transcendental Meditation teacher, Vale Hamilton, who is now a born again Christian, also describes her own experiences in Meditation: "As my consciousness extended, I became aware of the presence of spirit beings sitting on either side of me when I was meditating, and sometimes at night, they would sit on my bed. I spent three months meditating from three to ten hours a day. I had vivid experiences of demonic oppression while there. In the night during sleep, I woke with a sense of fear and apprehension as pressure was being put all over my head and body by a spirit who was trying to enter my body... I did not consider the possibility of Satan and his demons at that time, but just accepted it as a really weird trip... I even mistook them for guardian angels at times."

Surely, Christians do meditate on the Word of God; but Christian meditation must never be mistaken for Transcendental Meditation in all Christless religions and cults.

God has given man the privilege to be in control of his mind. But when man tries to run away from the realities of life by psychic practices, he opens his mind to demonic influence, to the prince of the power of the air. He is no longer in control of himself all the time. He gets 'possessed'. Unless he is soundly converted to Christ and able to renounce such practices and be prayed for and receive total deliverance, these demonic forces will continue to influence his life till he dies.

Most occultists come in contact with what most of them call 'the being of light' during their meditations, especially during their 'astral travels'. This 'being of light' is referred to by different names in different cults. He is the 'ECK' in the Eckankar Movement, the 'Das' or 'Krishna' in Hare Krishna Consciousness. Some other popular mystical organisations like the Rosicrucian (AMORC) call him 'the angel of light'. Some even regard such a being as the 'Grand Master Jesus'!!

According to the Bible, these beings are that same old liar and deceiver or some of his angels assigned for that purpose:

"And no marvel; for Satan himself is transformed into an angel of light. Therefore it is no great thing if his ministers (servants) also be transformed as the ministers of righteousness; whose end shall be according to their works." (2 Corinthians 11:14-15).

The question again is: With whom did Mohammed come in contact during his meditations? We have all the necessary material from Islamic sources to work on. Such records must be interpreted in the light of Scripture and judged by the Spirit of God.

Is Mohammed Not A Prophet?

Whatever their various spiritual and physical manifestations, there are only two spiritual forces working in the world today, namely, *"the Spirit of Truth"*, and *"the father of lies"* (John 16:13; 8:44). ANY spiritual experience that does not come from the Holy Spirit of the Bible, is from the 'father of lies'.

Some still wonder whether indeed Mohammed can be regarded as a prophet. From what we know of the man and his life, I believe Mohammed was a prophet.

Now, what is a prophet? The English word 'prophet' has its root in the Greek word 'pro' which means 'in place of', and 'phemi', which means 'speaking'. It is from the former that we have the English word 'pronoun', that is, a word used 'in place of' a noun. It is from 'phemi' we have the suffix of 'blasphemy' which means 'bad or irreverent speaking against God.' A prophet, therefore, means a person who speaks for or in place of another,

159

especially, a god (Exodus 7:1-2). Such a person may receive words directly from the god or God, or sometimes he can simply be inspired to speak or act. The prophecy could relate to current events or the foretelling of future events. What is important is that the person is being inspired by a power higher than himself.

It would be wrong therefore to imagine that Mohammed was not a prophet. From the story of his life and the realities of the religion of Islam, one should believe that Mohammed was a prophet, even a prophet of Allah.

But whether or not his Allah is the same God Almighty, the holy and triune God that reveals Himself to all the prophets in the Bible, is the subject of our debate here. We must not be afraid to discuss this because our very salvation depends on the understanding we have in this regard. If the Allah of Mohammed is the real God and his words are true, and the words in the Quran are his words, then all Bible believing Christians can be sure they are lost. On the other hand, if he is a demonic spirit masquerading as God Almighty, then every truth-seeking Muslim must consider this matter very seriously.

The Scripture says we should test the spirits behind all those who claim to be prophets in order to know what class they belong to. This testing or trying is defined in the Bible. But if we have a morbid fear of blasphemy, we will never be able to try a supposed spirit of God. Such a fear has led to serious bondage and to the deceiving of a great number of people resulting in eternal damnation. Every man is personally responsible to God for whatever he chooses to believe. God has given us a standard to judge all claims of spiritual

160

experiences. That is why Muslims must be quiet and let us do the probing together here.

The Nature Of Mohammed's Vision

The Arabic word "qur'an" means 'recitation'. And that is the reason why the messages in the Quran are regarded as the words of Allah as dictated to Mohammed piece by piece in his visions. It is these visions as visions of God upon which hangs the faith of 800 million Muslims.

All the evidence of plagiarism of Jewish tradition and folktales not withstanding, the Quran cannot be said to be simply a wholesale documentation of such traditions. We do believe that Mohammed indeed had some supernatural encounters, at least at the initial stage of his mission. We cannot explain this away, because in the Hadith we have a documentation of his deeds and experiences as testified by those who were close to him and were active in Islam during his time.

If he had no such experiences, he would not be a prophet but a philosopher. It is true he had friends who were acquainted with the Christian, Jewish and Zoroastrian religions, and copied some of their traditions (e.g. the use of beads in prayer), but Mohammed certainly had some spiritual experiences before he established his own religion. According to the narratives we have in the Hadiths, Mohammed did have visions.

The traditions that are referred to in this regard are those held reliable both by the Shi'ites and Sunnis. This is a very crucial area, and it is important to stress again that these stories were not cooked up by some Western historians to prove any point, but were written down by Muslims themselves. These are the testimonies of Ibn Ishaq, Husain ibn Muhammad, Ibn Athir, Muslim, Abu

Huraira, Al Bukhari, and even Zaid ibn Thabit, the Scribe of Mohammed and the traditional editor of the Standardized Quran.

According to these witnesses, often when 'the Inspiration' came upon Mohammed, he would fall to the ground, with his body shaking violently, perspiring intensively, eyes shut, mouth foaming and the face looking like that of a young camel. Sometimes, he would hear a bell ringing in his ears. The experience was normally followed by the most severe headaches. Abu Huraira is quoted in the Hadith as saying: "..when Inspiration descended on the Apostle, they used to bathe his sacred head with henna, because of the headache that used to come on."[2] However not on all occasions were the experiences so serious. Sometimes, he just simply appeared intoxicated. Muhammad Haykal records that when Mohammed's wife, Aisha, was accused of adultery, Mohammed received a revelation that was "accompanied by the usual convulsion"[3] to exonerate that wife.

It is worth noting here that Mohammed was very sincere with himself at first and suspected he might be under the influence of a demon. For example, why should he feel as if he were being strangled if it was a good God that wanted to give him a message? Must he be having such serious convulsions and fits before receiving a message from God? How are these different from what happen in some idolatrous rituals?

His guardian-wife Khadija seemed to have exacerbated the confusion. She and her uncle were the people who most influenced Mohammed at this

2 Cited in Pfander, C.G. *Mizzanul al-Haqq* (The Balance of Truth) Light of Life, Villach, Austria (1986) p.346

3 The Mizan'l Haqq Haykal, M. *'The Life of Mohammad'* p.337

critical moment of his life. When Mohammed started receiving his revelations, Khadija's cousin Waraqah ibn Nawfal was quoted as saying "...O Khadija, this must be the great spirit that spoke to Moses. Muhammad must be the Prophet of this nation. Tell him he must be firm."[4] She therefore encouraged him to submit to these experiences which they believed must be coming from the angel Gabriel. Khadija, said to be a member of one of the heretical Christian sects of those days, knew something about Gabriel and felt it must have been the angel giving Mohammed his messages. Similar events are recorded in Mishkat al Masabih, Sh. M. Ashraf (1990) pp.1252-1257. After the initial experiences, however, Mohammed became so fully possessed and convinced by the quranic message that he could recite it anywhere, any time. How did Waraqah, living in the time of the Nestorian and Arian heresies, know for sure that the spirit strangling Mohammed "**must**" be the same as that which spoke to Moses? These were the people that contributed to the confusion of Mohammed.

Even the idolaters of Mecca suspected something must be wrong somewhere. This is one of the reasons why they rejected his messages. They called him a *Majnun*, that is, "a poet possessed" (Surah 37:35-36; 68:2; 44:14; 52:29; 81:22, A.J. Arberry). He was also called *mashur*, that is, someone acting or speaking as a medium of evil spirits (Surah 25:8; 17:47; 81:22 etc). In at least eleven places, the Quran tries to defend Mohammed as not being possessed by demons. The existence of such excuses in the Quran proves that there were such strange experiences that there were suspicions among the people.

Before Mohammed was born, however, the Apostle John, writing by the inspiration of the Holy

4 ibid p.77

163

Spirit, had warned: *"Beloved, believe not every spirit, but try the spirits whether they are of God: because many false prophets are gone out into the world. Hereby know ye the Spirit of God: Every spirit that confesses that Jesus Christ is come in the flesh is of God: and every spirit that confesseth not that Jesus Christ is come in the flesh is not of God: and this is that spirit of antichrist, whereof ye have heard that it should come;"* (1 John 4:1-3).

Muhammad Marmaduke Pickthall, in the introduction to his translation of the Quran, says "Khadija tried the spirit". We ask: By what criteria did Khadija try the spirit behind Mohammed? When the Apostle John said people should "try the spirits", he was talking to those who knew the truth, those who were already in the light and had the standard for such trying and judging. But in the case of Khadija, as we have learnt from Muslim historians and as we pointed out in Chapter Eleven, she was a regular client of the idol priests in Mecca, despite her Christian background. When her sons were dying, she was consulting idols for divination and making sacrifices to them. How could such a person "try the spirit" influencing Mohammed to know its origin?

Waraqah who joined Khadija to encourage Mohammed did not live long enough to see how 'the great spirit' of Mohammed denied the deity of Christ. He died before Islam really took shape. The Arabian Christians at the time of Mohammed had no discernment of spirits because of their heresies and lack of true witness to Christ. They had not recovered from their backsliding when Islam engulfed the whole land like wild-fire and everybody was subjugated. The same tragedy looms over the Western world today if the Christians do not wake up.

The nature of the visions and inspiration of Mohammed is perhaps the most disturbing aspect of the history of Islam. Some writers ignore it because they do not see the significance; some deliberately remain silent to avoid any 'unpalatable' interpretation; and modern Muslim scholars, particularly, avoid the issue because of the implications, even though they see it in their Hadith. It is dangerous for a Muslim to ignore this area and not think properly about it.

As Christians, we cannot shrink from citing as well as interpreting any event in history to bring out a spiritual truth. Some well disposed Christian writers have suggested that one should avoid any detailed discussion when it comes to that aspect of the religion. They say that even though the historical facts may be given by the early Muslim historians themselves, we should talk of other things and not emphasize the nature of Mohammed's visions. The reason they give is that the conclusion from such will be offensive to Muslims, and will eventually prevent them from being converted. We should be objective, they say. And by that, they mean we should either be completely silent about it or mention it only passively if we must mention it at all. All we should concern ourselves with in Islam is the focus on the teachings and practices, and how these teachings fall short of providing salvation for man.

Proponents of this view, no doubt, have good intentions. But we need to understand that it is the origin that matters in things, especially, in spiritual things. We cannot improve a thing that had a wrong beginning. That is why Jesus told Nicodemus, *"Ye must be born again."* (John 3:7). He must begin from zero. What is wrong with Islam is not the teachings, as such, but the very source of the inspiration of the teachings.

As was said in Chapter One, the faith of the Muslim is firmly based on the belief that Mohammed had a revelation and visions from Allah and was reciting word for word what Allah told him to say. It is that faith that makes Islam. 'Islam' means 'submission to the will and words of Allah'. Remove that belief and there would be nothing called Islam. If, therefore, we are content with writing volumes on the doctrines and do not examine the source of the doctrines, we would miss the whole point. And this can be dangerous because we would give the impression that nothing is particularly wrong in Islam except the violence and certain doctrines. If we take such a stand, we would not be helping those who are sincere in their religion and would be ready to change if they could know the truth. We would tend to give them the impression that we are serving the same God with differences only in our worship systems and points of emphasis. Such a stand is delusive.

The aim of this book, therefore, is not to urge the Muslim reader to try and improve his character and turn over a new leaf or start a new sect of Islam. No! The problem is not with the leaf or even the fruit, but with the tree itself; the very seed was a wrong seed! (Matthew 12:33).

So, what is wrong with Islam is more than the doctrine; it is the inspirer of the basic doctrine; it is the very god whose spirit possessed Mohammed that has the big question mark.

But whoever the Allah was that had spoken to Mohammed at Hira, the true God still had a way of reaching out to the prophet. First, Khadija and Waraqa, though they did not have good Christian testimonies, had a Christian background, and would have informed Mohammed more about the stories of the Bible after his initial experiences.

Secondly, Mohammed had trade contacts with many Christians and Jews and must have learnt some things about the Bible and the Christian faith through them.

Moreover, when Khadija died, Mohammed married other wives who would have influenced his spiritual understanding if he wanted to learn more about the Gospel. One of his early wives was a Jewess called Raihana. His ninth wife, Safiyya, was also a Jewess whom he had captured after killing her husband in his battle against the Khaibar Jews. The then governor of Egypt, Moqawqa, presented to him two Ethiopian Christian slave ladies, Maryam and her sister Sirin. He took the senior sister as wife. So, in his household alone, Mohammed had two Christian and two Jewish witnesses. While the Jews would have explained the Old Covenant of God with Israel, the two Christians would have explained the New Testament of grace and reconciliation through Jesus.

All these were opportunities that Mohammed could have used to know the truth about God and the Bible.

But instead of establishing his faith on the true gospel stories that he could have collected from these people, he collected the stories in bits and shreds, mixed them with the ones he had heard during his caravan journeys, got inspired by a certain spirit, and then concocted his own fictions to build his new religion.

The devil has always been busy roaming about seeking whom he might use to oppose the Gospel of Jesus Christ in any particular time of history. It seems he saw in Mohammed all he needed in order to exterminate Christianity, which at that time had become weak.

Moreover, because there were many Christians in Yathrib (which he later called Medina or 'city of refuge' after conquering the city), Mohammed and the people of Arabia had further opportunities to receive the gospel.

God's Love For The Arabians

It was not by accident that Christians were already in Arabia before the time of Mohammed. It was the perfect plan of God.

First, God had to make sure that every nation then 'under heaven' was represented on that glorious Pentecost morning in Jerusalem when the Church of Jesus Christ was born.

It was impossible for just a handful of disciples to go to all the world to spread the gospel with no modern means of communication and transportation. But since Jews were already scattered among all the nations, God had to use them by bringing many of them as representatives from all these nations of the world to witness the birth of the Church of Christ, receive the gospel in its freshness and then go (back) into **all** the world and preach the gospel to every creature. Verse 11 of The Acts of The Apostles Chapter 2 says Arabians were right there on that occasion! And they were among the 3,000 individuals that heard about the wonderful works of God each "in his own language". When Peter preached the gospel these Arabs that believed, were baptised, and were immediately promised the same gift of the Holy Spirit that the disciples received that day! (verse 38).

All these people went back home, and we can be sure that the Arabs among them began to spread the gospel in their own land in that very first century.

Moreover, when the Roman persecution started and Jews were sent from Rome, some of them, including the Christians among them, fled to the Arabian Peninsula to continue their faith.

But many Arabs rejected the gospel and maintained their numerous gods until Allah, said to be one of the many, emerged to monopolise the scene under the human instrumentality of the energetic Mohammed with a promise to "fill Hell with the jinns and men all together." (Surah 11:119). And from there, the struggle began:

"Because that, when they knew God, they glorified him not as God, neither were thankful; but became vain in their imaginations, and their foolish heart was darkened ..who changed the truth of God into a lie, and worshipped and served the creature more than the Creator, who is blessed for ever. Amen....And even as they did not like to retain God in their knowledge, God gave them over to a reprobate mind, to do those things which are not convenient; Being filled with all unrighteousness, fornication, wickedness, covetousness, maliciousness: full of envy, murder, debate, deceit, malignity; whisperers, ..." (Romans 1:21, 25, 28-29).

At this juncture, every honest Muslim should be able to pray this prayer of the Quran: "Our Lord, we have wronged our own souls. If thou forgive us not and bestow not upon us Thy mercy, we shall certainly be lost." (Surah 7:23). The Bible says: *"How shall we escape if we neglect so great salvation;"* (Hebrews 2:3), offered by Christ Jesus?

It is pathetic that having succeeded in leading Mohammed astray and having fed him with enough gall of hatred for anything gospel, Allah instructed him to tell his followers that he did not know what would become of him or those following him after death (Surah 46:9). In other words, he was not sure if even he himself could reach the paradise of wine and women that he was preaching about!!

The Lord Jesus simply asks: *"Can the blind lead the blind? shall they not both fall into the ditch?"* (Luke 6:39).

And so here in Islam we have a perfect example of a religion without a redemption. And yet crowds of people, even respectable people, still follow!

The Bible speaks of *"a broad way that leadeth to destruction!"* It says, *"There is a way which seemeth right unto a man, but the end thereof are the ways of death."* (Proverbs 14:12).

Abu Huraria, in Mishkat al Masabih p.1118 said: "the Prophet summoned Quraish (his tribesman), and when they had gathered he addressed them in general and in particular saying. 'B. Ka 'b b. Lu 'ayy, deliver yourselves from hell; B. Murra b. K'ab, deliver yourselves from hell; B. 'Abd Shams, deliver yourselves from hell; B. 'Abd al-Muttalib, deliver yourselves from hell; Fatima, deliver yourselves from hell; for I have nothing which can avail you against God's punishment...".

"A'isha said that God's messenger used to say, 'O God, I seek refuge in Thee from the evil of what I have done..'". (ibid p.525). He is quoted by another witness, Abu Musa al-Ash'ari, "O God, forgive me my sin, my ignorance, my extravagance in my affairs and my frivolous sins, my unintentional and my intentional sins, for I am guilty of all that, O God, forgive me my former and my latter sins, what I have kept secret and what I have done openly" (ibid p.529).

What did he keep secret? Could it be the truths and discoveries about Jesus which he refused to tell the people? We do not know. All we know is that Mohammed had ignored God's salvation through Jesus Christ and established his own righteousness which had not been able to cater for his own sins. Since then, almost fourteen hundred years have passed by and billions of the souls of well meaning people have followed his religion and have passed away into eternity, *"without a hope, without God in this world."* I am terrified to imagine that number.

Mohammed probably had good intentions at the beginning, and desired to serve the true God. But he missed out somewhere along the line because he did not seem to meet a true Christian witness who would show him *"the Way, the Truth and the Life"*. If we Christians think deeply, we would realise how precious a soul is either in the hand of God or in the hand of the devil. If we refuse to witness to a sinner by our side, whose soul is hungry for God, do we know how far the devil can go with that soul if he fully possesses him? Men must be converted and be possessed with the Holy Spirit or else they will be diverted and...

The whole work of the devil on earth is to get as many people as possible to be with him in the Lake of Fire. In the Quran, Surah 11:119 which was referred to earlier, Allah (whoever he is) says: "I will fill hell with the jinns (demons) and men all together." This decision of the god of Islam is re-affirmed in Surah 7:177-178, and Surah 32:13.

A Muslim should not lose hope. We are happy to announce that there is a better God. *"For **God** (of the Bible) so loved the world (mankind) that he gave his only begotten Son, that whosoever believeth in Him should not perish (in hell) but have everlasting life (in the real heaven)."* (John 3:16).

Yet the individual Muslim should realise that even though Allah is capable of leading, and surely will lead, all those who follow him to hell as he has promised, if that Muslim takes his stand and repents TODAY, regardless of his position in Islam, Jesus will become the LORD of his life and he or she will become one of His sheep. As the Good

Shepherd, Jesus said: *"My sheep hear my voice, and I know them, and they follow me: And I give unto them* **eternal life;** *and they shall* **never perish,** *neither shall any man* (nor devil, nor strange god) *pluck them out of my hand. My Father, which gave them me, is greater than all; and* **no man** *is able to pluck them out of my Father's hand."* (John 10:27-29). Hallelujah!

This is the kind of Saviour we have in Christianity. The area that you as a Muslim may find extremely difficult to believe in the Bible, especially concerning the deity of Christ, is the very place where your salvation lies!

This book is certainly not for everybody. It is only for those who are not afraid to face the truth — those whose minds are large enough to reason and not get enraged when confronted with some hard facts that affect their present and eternal destiny. If you are a Muslim and have patiently read this book to this point, we are sure the Holy Spirit of God must have been doing the work of conviction of sin in your heart. But the choice is still yours: to receive your salvation now or never. Tomorrow will surely be too late for you to make up your mind. Allah has nothing to offer you other than charms, amulets, wives, and riches (without peace) that will end here on earth. Jesus said, *"For what is a man profited, if he shall gain the whole* world, *and lose his own soul?"* — in hell! (Matthew 16:26). You can't even gain the whole world!

Even if your whole family are Muslims, God has sent you this book because He wants to save you *"from your vain conversation* (worthless way of life) *received by tradition from your fathers;"* (1 Peter 1:18).

"And the times of this ignorance God winked at; but now commandeth **all men everywhere** (including the Muslim reader of this book) *to repent:"* (Acts 17:30). Or maybe you think those who will be in hell will

172

be those who have no religion? *"I tell you, Nay: but except ye repent, ye shall all likewise perish."* (Luke 13:3). Maybe you think the Lake of Fire will be filled with only the modern and traditional occultists, armed robbers and drug addicts? *"I tell you, Nay, but except ye **repent**, ye shall all likewise perish."* (Luke 13:5).

"While it is said, Today if ye will hear his voice, (even as you are hearing now) *harden not your hearts, as in the provocation."* (Hebrews 3:15).

Since you have been patient enough with me to read through to this point and have had the opportunity to know these facts, make up your mind and be ready for God's operations in your heart right now.

Go down on your knees NOW or find a lonely place and confess your sin of rebellion and ignorance, and ask the Lord JESUS CHRIST to cleanse you from all your sins by HIS BLOOD, and save you. You will not regret doing so, and you will never be the same again. Let me hear from you what God has done in your life. You will not be the first Muslim to be saved and you will not be the last! How long would you continue repeating the al Fatiha and yet not be sure of salvation? Many are coming to the true light and the true path and many more will see this light before the second coming of Jesus. You can be one of them!

GOD BLESS

174

APPENDIX

Background to Islam

Muslim Beliefs

Islam has five practical duties for all believers (the Pillars of Islam):

1. The Declaration of Faith (Shahada), that there is no god but Allah and Mohammed is Allah's messenger. This is proclaimed from the mosque at each call to prayer.

2. Five compulsory daily prayers (Salat). These are ritual prayers according to a prescribed pattern and said in the direction of Mecca.

3. Welfare contribution (Zakat). This is a compulsory payment for various community needs, including the poor.

4. Pilgrimage to Mecca (Hajj). This is the pinnacle of achievement in a Muslim's life and is intended to be accomplished at least once in a lifetime.

5. Fasting (Sawm). A fast for daylight hours during the ninth lunar month of Ramadan.

Jihâd is also prominent in the teaching of Islam though it is not normally included as one of the pillars. This is the struggle to advance Islam by all and any means, and is incumbent on all Muslims. Even though some Muslims do not consider Jihâd (striving with might or main) as a major pillar, yet the Quran itself states clearly in Surah 9:19 that there are three things that attract more rewards than all others. These are: belief in Allah, belief in the Last Day, and Jihâd. These supersede many other good deeds in Islam according to this portion of the Quran.

The Muslim faith includes belief in angels, both good and bad, belief in the 'Books of God' including the Torah, the Psalms, and the Gospels of the Bible although these are considered corrupted in their present form and also abrogated by the Quran, considered to be the final revelation of Allah. Also belief in prophets, including the Biblical prophets and Jesus, but majoring on Mohammed as the final prophet; belief in life after death and judgment day, although both of these are quite different from the Christian belief.

The Quran

The Quran is thought to have been transmitted piecemeal to Mohammed at various times, including times of need when certain decisions were to be made in the life of the community. It is considered to be Divine revelation and to be transmitted directly from Allah. The first revelation is said to have come via an angel when Mohammed was meditating in a cave. Later revelations were through many forms including visions and dreams, through angels, by direct communication from Allah and during a time when Mohammed was taken to Heaven in a rapture. It has 114 chapters, called Surahs, each divided into verses called Ayat (ayat is plural ≡ verses, ayah is singular ≡ verse). The Surahs are not in the chronological order in which Mohammed received them, nor do they follow a progressive historical arrangement. Scholars can detect two major periods when the Quran was thought to be revealed. These are associated with phases of Mohammed's life; in Mecca, and Medina. The Quran is not easy to read and there are apparent contradictions, which scholars seek to explain by the fact that later revelations abrogated (cancelled) certain earlier ones. The Quran was not collected during Mohammed's lifetime but scraps of information, checked by acceptable witnesses, were assembled from many sources by his followers after his death. Today many versions of the Quran exist although this is often denied. There is diversity in versification. For example, Surah 5 in Yusuf Ali's translation is split into 123 verses whereas in Al Hilali, Khan Muhsin and Mohammed Pickthall it is split into 120 verses. A Muslim is taught that the Quran is the final revelation from Allah and it is, therefore, treated with great honour and forms the basis of the Islamic religion. Along with the Hadith there is considered to be a complete code for all aspects of life.

The Hadith

As well as the teachings of the Quran, Muslims are taught from the Hadith. It was customary in Mohammed's time for the traditions of forefathers to be followed among families and tribes. This would apply to many aspects of life from simple things, like the way to walk or the way to tie one's sandals, to the more complex aspects of family and community life. Mohammed's followers were taught that they were to learn from their prophet and so the traditions have been passed down from generation to generation of how Mohammed would have carried on many aspects of everyday life. These are recorded in the volumes of the Hadith and are interpreted for each generation by the religious leaders of the Islamic communities.

Sunna(h)

This is a traditional portion of Mohammedan Law based on Mohammed's words or acts, but not

177

written by him, accepted as authorititive by the Orthodox and rejected by the Shiites.

Mohammed and the rise of Islam

Mohammed grew up in a society which was divided with many power and religious struggles. He was born in Mecca (in Arabia) in 570 AD, where there were many idols, cults and many different gods. Worship was centred on the Ka'ba (or Kabah), a large cubic stone structure covered with a black cloth. After Mohammed began to receive revelations he began to acquire followers and also some resistance, which caused him to flee to Medina, where Islam was established. His revelations gave him the status of a prophet and he became the religious, political and social leader of the community. Resistance to Islam arose, particularly from Mecca and a number of battles were fought, until finally Mohammed led his followers victoriously to take Mecca in 629 AD. Mohammed died in Medina in 632 AD. From that point Islam moved forward very quickly taking hold of one community after another, chiefly by the sword. Since then it has grown to nearly one thousand million people across the whole world. A number of internal conflicts have separated off several Islamic sects, the chief of which are the Sunni and Shi'a sects.

No truly Islamic nation is democratic and none has ever been so. In those Islamic nations where the democratic system is in operation it is seen as a necessary evil enforced upon the nation by the Western world. No freedom of expression or worship exists in any Islamic nation.

No freedom of of expression or worship exists in any truly Islamic nation.

SELECTED BIBLIOGRAPHY

Abd-Al-Masih, *Islam Under the Magnifying Glass*, Light of Life, Austria.

Al-Hilali (et al), *Holy Qur'an: Explanatory English Translation*, Hilal Publications, Ankara, Turkey.

Alli, A.Yusuf, *The Qur'an: Text, Translation and Commen tary*

CAN (Kaduna), *Kaduna Religious Riot '87: A Catalogue of Events.*

Bernard Lewis (ed), *Islam: From Prophet Mohammed to the Capture of Constantinople,* Vol. 1 Vol. Politics and War, Macmillan (USA), 1974.

Christy, J.W *Introducing Islam,* Friendship Press, N.Y

Cragg, K. *The Call of the Minaret,* Daystar Press, Ibadan (1988)

Dashti, Ali, *23 Years: A Study of the Prophetic Career of Mohammed,* George Allen & Unwin, London, (1974).

Dawood, J. *The Qur'an: Translation,* Penguin Books, N.Y.

Deedat, A. *What Is His Name?* Islamic Centre.

Fry, G., & King, R.,*Islam: A Survey of the Muslim, Faith,* Baker Books House, G.R. Michigan (1982)

Gatje, Helmut. *The Qur'an And Its Exegesis,* Routledge and Kegan Paul, London (1976).

Gibbs, Levi-Provencial, Schacht, *Encyclopædia of Islam,* Leiden: J. Brill, (1913).

Gilchrist, John. *Evidences for the Collection of the Qur'an,* Jesus to the Muslims, Benoni, South Africa (1984).

Guillaume, A. *The Life of Muhammad* O.U.P London (1975). [This is a translation and combination of the two earliest. most reliable biographies of Mohammed titled The Life History of Muhammad by Ibn Ishaq (A.D.768) and The Expeditions of Muhammad by Al-Waqidi (A.D.822)].

Hanua, M. *The True Path: Seven Muslims Make Their Greatest Discovery*, International Doorways Publishers, Colorado (1975).

Haykal, M.H. *The Life Muhammad*

Hoballah, Dr Mahmoud, *Muhwmmad The Prophet*, The Islamic Centre, Washington D.C.

Hodgson, Marshall. *The Order of Assasins*, Mouton & Co., Grevenhage (1955).

Hughes, T., A *Dictionary of Islam*, Allen & Co., London 1885

Ibn Ishaq, *Sirat'ul Rasool*, Ibn Hisham (Ed). Oxford University Press (1955).

Jadeed, Iskander, *The Infallibility of the Torah and the Gospel*, The Good Way, Rikon, Switzerland.

Jeffery, A. *Islam: Muhammad and His Religion*, Bobbs-Merrill, Indianapolis (1958).

Jeffery, A., *Foreign Vocabulary of the Qur'an*, Al-Biruni, Lahore (1977)

Khan Dr, Muhsin Muhammed (ed). *Al Bukhari*, Nazi Publications, 121 Fulquarmain Chambers, Granpat Road, Lahore, Pakistan, 6th Ed., 1986. Selected portions of this Hadith are also reproduced in Muhsin Khan et al. English translation of the Quran.

Laffin, John, *The Dagger of Islam*, Sphere Books, London (1979).

Lamb, David, *The Arabs* Random House, N.Y (1987).

Lings, Martin, *Muhammad. His Life Based on the Earliest Sources*, Islamic Texts Society, London (1983).

Lukhoo, Sir Lionel, *The Qur'an is not the Word of God*, Lukhoo Ministries, Texas.

Marsh, Charles, *The Challenge of Islam* (formerly *Too Hard for God?*), Scripture Union, London.

Miller, M. William, *A Christian Response To Islam*, Presbyterian and Reformed, London (1976).

Morey, Robert, *The Islamic Invasion*, Harvest House Publication, Oregon (1992).

Muhammad, Maulana Ali, *A Manual of Hadith*, The Ahmadiyya Anjuma, Ishatt Islam n.d. Lahore.

Muir, W., *The Life of Mohammad*, John Gran, Edinburgh (1923).

Nehls, Gerhard, *Christians answer Muslims*, SIM International/Life Challenge, Belville (1988).

Pfander, C.G., *The Balance of Truth (The Mizanu'l Haqq)* [enlarged], Light of Life, Víllach, Austria (1986).

Pickthall, M. Marmaduke, *The Meaning of the Glorious Koran*, Islamic Publications Bureau, Lagos.

Prayers of the Prophet (with Arabic text, compiled and translated by A.H. Farid). Sh. Muhammad Ashraf Publications, Lahore.

Robson, James, *Mishkat al Masabih*, Sh. Muhammad Ashraf Publications, 1990. Originally by Immam Hussain al-Baghawi, The Book House, Lahore.

Rodwell, J.M., *The Koran*, Everyman's Library.

Shorrosh, Anis, *Islam Revealed. A Christian Arab's View of Islam*, Thomas Nelson, Nashville, (1980).

Siddiqt, Abdul Hadid, *Sahih Muslim*, Sh. Muhammad Ashraf Publications, Pakistan (1987).

Smith, Jane, *An Historical and Semitic Study of the Term Islam as seen in a Sequence of Qur'an Commentaries*, University of Montana for Harvard University Dissertations (1970).

Tisdal, W. St. Clair. *Christian Reply to Muslim Objections*, Light of Life, Villach (1980).

Tisdal, W. St.Clair. *The Original Sources of the Qur'an*, SPCK., London (1905).

Zwemer, Samuel, *The Moslem Doctrines of God: An Essay on the Character and Attributes of Allah to the Koran*, American Tract Society, New York (1905).

NOTES